Lessons from the Round Pen

By Harriet Sabatini

Illustrated by Clare, Lara & Bernard Sabatini

© 2010 by Bezalel Books

Published by
Bezalel Books
Waterford, MI
www.BezalelBooks.com

Printed in the United States of America

ISBN 978-0-9844864-5-8
Library of Congress Control Number 2010935333

OTHER BOOKS BY HARRIET SABATINI

Joseph's Hands

Las Manos de José

Isabel's Sister

# My Flight

I want to fly

Beyond my reach

Beyond the scope

Of my endurance.

And dance in the moonlight

Swift and sure

Wild and free.

Lord I want to

Leap and laugh and shout

Till all within tumbles out

Sprawling haywire on dewy grass

And never, never

Let the moment pass!


I want to fly

Beyond my reach

Peering down

Above the blue and green hill's crown.

Touch the stars

And never think of coming down.

Lord I want to

Soar and spring about

Till all within tumbles out

So topping this cloud swept height

Find your open arms

Within my flight!

H.S.

To Charles, Janice and Heather

A perfect blend of God and horses!

And

The indomitable, loveable Sr. Chris

And

Mark Lowe, DVM

The Best Veterinarian and friend ever

## Introduction

Ever since I could put two thoughts together it has been about God and horses. Don't mistake me: God is the most important and I am privileged to dwell in His grace and by His grace. However, it was not until well into my adult life that I realized my passion for horses was His gift to me. At many crossroads in my life a horse has been there to meet me. Each time the encounter brought into my life a fuller understanding of God's love. Even in my youth, the Lord was preparing me to come into a closer relationship and patiently waiting for me to learn His language.

When Max came into my life, God took my love for this strange, stubborn, misunderstood animal to show me how I looked to Him. This is our story and it is written for one purpose only: to tell you how much God loves you. So, I suppose it is a love story. All of creation is God's gift to us and it coaxes us to believe in the beauty and goodness of the Creator. Just think about the poetry of the horse. Long limbed, graceful, powerful and willing to be our friend – a winning combination that is tough to beat.

If it wasn't for Pat Parelli's Natural Horsemanship program that got my feet wet and taught me the horse's language I would still be a dumb, blind human. I thank him for teaching me and also teaching me how to figure things out. Horses are individuals and for every truth I learned, Max challenged me to think outside the box. There are **many** great horse teachers out there today that are revolutionizing the horse world.

Charles and Janice Hall and their daughter Heather are all that is best in the horse and people world. Wisdom, Caring, Intuitiveness and Courage are the least of their gifts and they have shared them with me over the years so that I can love my horses more fully. Charles fixed Max's terrible hoof problems and gave him eight more years of life free of painkillers. They continue to inspire me.

To the horse expert, this book will reveal my ignorance. I am not nor ever will be a "horse whisperer". You will see simple solutions to the problems that bewildered me. And most likely you will see how adroit Max was at keeping one step ahead of my knowledge. This book is about a God/child relationship and in no way designed to teach horsemanship.

I wasn't expecting God to use natural horsemanship to reach me. I wasn't expecting Him to love me so unconditionally. As Max began to trust me and look to me for his happiness, I likewise took a page from his book and saw the Lord the same way. And if my experiences can open your hearts just a little to the bountiful love of Jesus then I am humbly thankful.

Many don't prescribe to religion these days. And religion has had a bad rap in many regards. But God is unchangeable truth and to top it off He is interested in your happiness! Why, I don't know.....but He is. That was my big surprise. He would never give up on me much the same way I doggedly spent ten years trying to fix Max, understand Max, and have a relationship with him. Like my horse, I was broken, misunderstood and stubborn (not to mention selfish and self-protecting). Yet the Lord Jesus has never given up on me and my freedom.

The round pen is life. We all have to leave it at one point. The way out is the center where love, comfort and eternal happiness wait to embrace us.

Harriet Sabatini, MCA
Marygate Farm in Trinity, Alabama
June 30, 2010

A round pen is a useful training space if you have the room for one. Usually measuring 55-66 feet in diameter, the pen serves as a safe place to turn out young horses and provides a smaller space to work a horse from the ground as well as in the saddle.

For training young or very excitable horses, a breaking pen with a 35-foot diameter and solid, 7-foot high walls provides a place to work with no distractions. A fractious horse can't climb over the walls, but there's no quick way out for the trainer either.

Taken from *Horse and Rider Gear's Glossary of Horse Terms and Definitions*
(http://www.horseandridergear.com)

## Lesson 1 – Revelation

The pleasant spring morning greeted me as I guided my horse Max down the wooded path. The frost gently melted as the hot sun surfaced the horizon. Breathing smoke, Max charged ahead.

We trotted along in perfect agreement until we reached the large field. Then the fight began. This was an ongoing dialog about our workout plans. His idea of an outing was to trot around the field once and head back to his comfortable pasture. My preference was to practice circles, enjoy a few gallops and run figure eights around the hay rolls. I had the reins so Max grudgingly complied. Every time we reached the exit lane to the field, I waged a ferocious battle to keep him from darting back to the barn. Today, the argument quickly reached a climax.

Uppermost in my mind was that I had little time to ride before work. Did I even ride for pleasure anymore?

No, that had ceased long ago. My relationship with Max was reduced to combat tactics every time I took him away from his stall.

Momentarily triumphant, we galloped around the perimeter once again. The path beckoned. This time the planets all lined up. Max tried to turn but I was ready for him. As I countered his movement he gave a vigorous buck. I was momentarily off balance. Max took his chance, gave another huge buck and I flew into the air. The wet grass rose up to meet me as my horse sped away with thundering hooves.

"Whoa Max!" I yelled at his furiously retreating form. (It was a lengthy walk to the barn.)

To my utter amazement he stopped and looked over his shoulder with a mocking eye. I felt rather than saw his delight as he quickly disappeared down the path. Rehearsing threats, I picked myself up and began my long trek to the barn.

"It's not fair. All I ask of this horse is one or two hours a day. In return he gets a stall of his own, top quality feed, chiropractic care, a field to graze in, horse buddies and all the supplements I can afford." I gritted my teeth – it *wasn't* too much to ask him for one hour out of the twenty four.

Being thrown by my horse brought me swiftly to the pinnacle of my discontent. Riding boots are not made for long walks! I trudged on with plenty of time to evaluate the growing abyss between Max and myself. It was painfully obvious that after five years my horse did not like or even respect me. I needed to find him a new home. Due to disabilities, Max could not be sold on the general market. I began to consider the options for his future with a heavy heart. I was going to get out of horses altogether – so complete was my disillusionment and failure.

God's sense of humor always amazes me. He had other plans. My first lesson in the round pen commenced. I kept meeting my tail as I ran around the circle. Failure and frustration nibbled at my ego. Max resented me more each day. Perhaps he would be good at a farm that dealt with disabled children. As I thumbed through my mail that evening, a brochure that described "Natural Horsemanship" appeared. With small but persistent hope I read the literature. Deep inside me the longing to know my horse and communicate with him leapt up at the promises. Through a series of events I enrolled myself in this self help program. Maybe I could become a *horse whisperer*! I didn't realize at the time God was enrolling me in a program of His own. The communication had finally begun.

The first thing I learned was that an hour a day *was* too much to ask of Max. Actually a minute or second of coercion was too much. Max didn't care two hooves about the expensive supplements, the wonderful stall, the field, or my affectionate massages. What Max wanted was respect and communication. He didn't understand or want to understand English – so I had to learn his language. Horses speak with their bodies. As I studied this, I did not know it was my passport to learning the language of God.

Our heavenly Father knew that the "good things" in life were not what I wanted. The perfect horse, great equestrian skills, and the courage to acquire them were only things. Max was looking for a relationship of respect. Deep down inside that is what I sought as well. Much of my relationship with God had to do with my *success* as a Christian. But God didn't want performance; He wanted a loving relationship.

Up until this point, my form of communication with Max was typical of the inexperienced, bull headed human. I put a bit in his mouth and spurs on my boots. These reinforced the master slave relationship and confirmed in my horse's mind that I was no different from any other human he encountered. I completely misunderstood the horse psyche. My idea was to "show him who's boss" and to win every battle. I had confused leadership with being "boss". Somehow I think my relationship with God was like that: "I am a good Christian if I let God win every battle". What kind of boss was God?

In short order the horsemanship course opened my eyes to what goes on in the horse's mind. For instance, I learned that horses are prey animals and humans are predators. Eyes in the front and straight line approaches mean the human is coming to "eat" the horse. My natural body language was a threat. So preconceived notions were put aside as well as much of what I had been previously taught. It was difficult physically and mentally to learn to use prey animal body language. However, once I put it into practice, Max became a different animal. I knew I had found partnership to replace conflict.

Shortly after this 'Epiphany', I attended a retreat to spend some time with the Lord. Typically, I avoid retreats like the plague. It is every bit as stressful as being ridden by a dumb human. Perhaps I didn't like looking at my life. I never liked what I saw. So I clenched my teeth to get through it and faked some relevancy. This time, during the priest's talk an earthquake took place in my heart. Quite simply, it was breaking. As soon as the talk ended, I rushed out into the warm spring day.

Some supernatural force drove me. I couldn't even see where I was going. I reached the edge of the woods with my hand clutched to my chest. I was trying to hold the pieces of my heart together. God was communicating with me. He was using my budding horse knowledge on me to do so!

Horses love to be stroked with soft touches. They love attention, grooming, and a feeling of safety when they are around you. The confident and cheerful touch creates a comfort zone for them. They want to be near you. Also, to speak to a horse requires a thorough knowledge of how he moves his body.

Once I began to read the flick of Max's ears or the way he snaked his neck, among other postures, I knew what he was saying. Immediately, I experienced the connection in my Christian walk. The Lord saw my passion for horses as a pathway into the very depths of my soul. He was pleased with my efforts to love and serve Him; however, these efforts would not carry me beyond a fundamental fear of God himself.

As I said, the earth was breaking away from my heart. My little bit of spading around the fig tree was not bearing fruit. God allowed my heart to break into great chunks of weedy earth.

And God said to me, "How do you look at ME?"

I replied, "You have spurs on your boots and a whip in your hand. But you love me...."

"And?"

"I am stuck in the arena doing exercise after exercise. But only for an hour...you don't ask too much..."

And beneath the earthy clumps that had crumbled I felt the hands of God stroking my fleshly heart. Yes, there was a real heart in there – not the one I had created. And He had no whip or spur – none were needed to advance his Kingdom. Subservience was not what He desired. He wanted to love me. Now that my connection with Max helped me understand mutual respect, the Lord used it to teach me about His own respect for me. My dutiful service never fostered a love relationship. God was inviting me to learn His language to fulfill my deepest human longings. The idea that He would respect me took my breath away. What? The Lord of the Universe *cared* enough to direct the course of my life through a horse!

There are many teachers helping us amateurs learn to respect the horse. I thank them for horses have much to teach us. To speak body language, to quit acting like the predator horses instinctively know us to be, means a total change in body, mind and soul. We must become as much like them as we can. We put ourselves in their hooves, so to speak. Sounds like something someone else did in order to bring us to Himself.

So my first lesson in the round pen concluded. As Max approached me with relief and wondering eyes, my new partnership proceeded with joy. As I realized that my failures and accomplishments did not interest God, my partnership with Him matured. My dignity as a human person created in His image was and is His gift. In fact, He was willing to die for it. The invitation was to love and respect in return. The more patient and merciful a god I became for my horse, the more I began to plumb the depth of the infinite patience and mercy of the God who loved me.

Questions to Ponder:

1. What does your idea of God look like?
2. Does God love me more for what I can do or who I am?
3. Would I let Him stroke my heart?  How do I self-protect?
4. How do I feel that God communicates with me?
5. Do I have a passion in my life that can be utilized by God to better my relationship with Him?

## The Spirit to Know You

Gracious and Holy Father, Please give me: intellect to understand you, reason to discern you, diligence to seek you, wisdom to find you, a spirit to know you, a heart to meditate upon you, ears to hear you, eyes to see you, a tongue to proclaim you, a way of life pleasing to you, patience to wait for you and perseverance to look for you. Grant me a perfect end, your holy presence, a blessed resurrection and life everlasting.

### St Benedict of Nursia

## Lesson 2 – Healing

The Retreat continued. God was not finished. In fact, He had just begun. Time seemed suspended. Later, I was to find that two hours had gone by – and lunchtime! This was really tragic as they have epic food at this retreat center.

Part of the journey Max and I had undertaken involved healing. In order to function, Max was regularly dosed with painkillers by his previous owner. His feet were three sizes too small for a horse of his dimensions. Early shoeing had bound his feet. Because of this and a history of unbalanced trimming, his hoof structure had been compromised. Pain forced him to compensate, which set up a chain reaction of stiffness in his whole body. The old adage says, "No feet, no horse" and at fourteen years of age I witnessed that in spades. I quit giving him the drug once I found out that its use actually leached vital fluids from his already painful joints. Thus began a four year quest to cure him of his lameness. It took time, Herculean effort, tears, gadgets and lots of money. I consulted with different farriers. I consulted with different veterinarians. I was resigned to keep him comfortable with herbal remedies, chiropractic care and exercise.

Then, as grace would have it, while auditing a natural horsemanship seminar, I met a woman who happened to be a farrier. She traveled, gypsy-like, all over the land plying her trade. (Except that she drove a van instead of ponies harnessed to a cart!) Once I explained my horse's problem, she exclaimed, "Why honey, you've got to take them shoes off!"

All the expert advice I had ever received involved 'fixing' Max with corrective shoeing. This was a new concept indeed.

Subsequently, she proceeded to educate me on the function of the hoof. Hooves, by design, expand and contract under the weight and movement of the horse. Not only does this action help blood circulate through the horse's body, it keeps the hoof healthy and strong. Shoes prevent the hoof from performing this natural function. This is not an attack on the practice of shoeing horses. I never intend to write that book. But I did learn enough to be convinced that in Max's case, his shoes should be removed. She also convinced me to find someone who understood the hoof enough to trim my horse correctly. I believe it was God who led me to a wonderful couple who have taught me a lot more than just the physics of the hoof!

So Max's shoes came off and he started the restorative trimming that his hooves needed. Max started this life journey at seventeen. At twenty four, he was eighty five percent restored (and just as ornery as ever). Years of damage (including my own ignorance) would only allow that much.

Meanwhile, at the retreat, still under the influence of the Divine Presence, I went to the old chapel on the grounds. This preserved chapel of Blessed Trinity Shrine Retreat represents the Catholic presence in Southern Alabama from the early nineteen hundreds. Many men and women lived and worshipped here in total commitment to the Lord. It is a holy place – I mean a *holy* place. As I entered, I knelt at the foot of the altar. At once, I experienced a still small voice say, "Take off your shoes, this is holy ground". As I bent to remove my shoes another wave of realization knocked the breath right out of me. As I had removed Max's shoes, so God was removing mine. And what did that mean?

Trembling with awe as the Lord intervened; I humbly acknowledged His love and graciousness toward me. He was serious! He was reaching down from heaven to repair our relationship.

Immediately, I was struck by the passage in scripture where Jesus says that you don't put patches on old wineskins because they will burst – no - new wineskins were for new wine! I felt at that moment as if my old wineskin had burst – and all the old vinegar poured out. And it drained all my preconceived notions of what constituted the Christian life. No, God did not want to patch me up – new wineskins! For the first time I understood that passage.

A horseshoe holds the hoof rigid. The shoe forces the foot to expand upward – the exact opposite of the way God designed it. Shoes also prevent blood circulation in the hoof. Reduced blood flow can create pockets of dead matter inside the foot. I believe it is akin to having feet that always feel a little bit numb. Shoes do not provide better traction either. In fact, they make the going more slippery on pavement and other hard surfaces. All his life Max was doing incredible athletic feats with this handicap! No wonder he hurt.

Like a hoof with a shoe, my own Christian life was handicapped. My approach was to concentrate on self-correction. Once I was presentable, I could approach the throne. Constant surveillance and failure formed dead pockets deep within my heart. As I trudged, cross in tow, up the mountainside, it was only natural that I would slip and tumble down life's slick surface. My life with Jesus was always a little bit numb.

So my 'horseshoes' were being removed. The Lord wanted me contracting and expanding normally – He wanted to restore circulation. I think that my 'horseshoes' contributed to my unhealthy fear of God. An irritating but commanding voice sat on my shoulder and whispered, "But it is not enough."

Deep in my heart I always worried about facing Jesus at my death and seeing disappointment on His face. Now, as He so gently and lovingly stripped away that long nurtured lie, I had no idea what the future held. However, I had one thing I could cling to: He loved me.

"What? How? What's next?" I whispered in the quiet chapel. I wanted all the answers and I wanted them *now*. My habitual controlling instinct insisted we start the process right away, according to *my* specifications. I had yet to learn to surrender control. For most of my life I reacted violently to the phrase, "Let go and let God". I was beginning to understand that letting go of my mistrust of Him would usher in the freedom He desired for me.

But our wise Lord said, "This is enough for now. As you learn from your horse, my teaching will make sense to you."

And through the following years this episode has repeatedly called me to faith. I realized that God had to remake me into His own image – into the person He had always intended for me to be. At the center of my version of the Christian life was a wounded, mistrustful, and frightened person. The iron shod control over my life had to end. As I removed my shoes, I began a relationship of trust in Jesus, the God/Man who would make me new. This was certainly good news! I began to anticipate becoming the person God desired me to be.

Whoa there! If you had asked Max what it felt like to be barefoot after a lifetime of shoes, he would have given you an earful. He tottered around his pasture feeling quite sorry for himself. As he couldn't be ridden at first, the hiatus was well spent being his friend. I was able to advance in all important ground work. Gone were the spurs, the agenda, the arena – time now for renewal and healing. He must grow new hooves over a series of years in order to have the feet God intended for him.

So my pink new skin was very raw. Max and I learned to grow new hooves together. Whenever I experience growth – painful awareness of sin and lack of trust in God – I use the phrase "Growing New Hooves". And then I get trimmed.

But it is exciting! Where I used to condemn myself and submit myself to 'rules', God's tenderness prompts in me a grateful yes, an eager yes, because I can see a new person emerging. My "English" is being replaced by God's body language – the cross! Breathtaking!

Father Judge's Chapel.                    Holy Trinity, Alabama.

Questions to Ponder:

1. What are my horseshoes?  What has shaped me in a way that God did not intend?  How is my will involved?

2. Am I afraid to have my shoes removed?  Am I afraid to undergo a complete change?

3. How do I react to God's interaction in my life?  Is it "please only a little bit at a time" or take the whole life?  Do I put constraints on how I let God change me?  How can I let go?

4. Removing Max's shoes was a painful process for him. Do I fear the pain of change?  Do I mistrust God's way and type of change?

# Lesson 3 - Forgiveness

With muddy clay plastered to my new riding boots, I had to admit it was a standoff. Earlier, Max and I traveled serenely down a steep ravine and encountered a small ditch. It had the remains of spring rains in its belly. Beyond were lovely wooded trails and pastures to explore. I anticipated a fun outing with my equine partner. As we approached the ditch, he threw up his head and planted his feet. At my urging, he inched closer and dropped flaring nostrils toward the murky water. He refused to cross. Undaunted, I tried to ride him over. When that yielded only trampled trees and sweaty brow, I dismounted and tried to lead him over. A shadow of foreboding hovered as I coaxed and pleaded. He set his feet, laid back his ears and rolled an eye at me.

I was ready to either (A) take a two by four to his head or (B) sell him to Alpo.

I actually informed him in no uncertain terms that A or B was going to happen. He hunched his shoulder and refused to budge. I begged him. I petted him. New to natural horsemanship, I thought I was being *very* patient. (At least *I* thought I was!) But it was to no avail.

My former training taught me to always finish what you start. I could not leave until I won. On that day I didn't win. Finally, three and a half hours later I tugged him up the ravine and stalked back to the barn. Max just looked down his patrician Roman nose and thought, "Good riddance!"

The vestiges of my former training still clung to my stubborn brain. I was learning that it helps to know the reasons behind a horse's behavior. Max didn't respect or trust me enough to cross that terrifying ditch. I remembered something I read about a horse's perspective. Their eyes are set wide apart for 360 degree vision. They are a prey animal and must be able to see a wide area. Their big forehead and nose stick out between their eyes. That ditch did look dangerous to him. My anger and impatience only confirmed his suspicions. I must have looked pretty fierce with mud splashed to the eyeballs and clenched teeth. He was probably thinking, "Wow, that was a close one!"

It is a good image of my own partnership with my soul. That ditch that is ever present as it taunts me to get across. What was the ditch? It was my fallen human nature. Hurts and betrayals of life skewed my perception. The harder I tried to get over it the bigger and scarier it became. As time went on I became like Max in many ways – ready to do anything but cross that ditch! My new relationship with God led me to the brink. As Max did not trust me to get past the 'abyss', I did not really trust the Lord to get me across my own failures.

To help me understand Max, I tried walking around with a big cup placed between my eyes. For us predators, whose eyes are in the front of our head, a cup makes it really hard to see straight. After knocking things over and bumping my head, I appreciated my horse's hesitation. I know my perception of God and myself blinded me to his urgings to move forward safely in His grace.

I began to ponder this blindness. Jesus healed many blind people. Some saw right away. Some took a few treatments. I asked God to show me my blindness and remove it. This is a lifelong journey. I must always be aware of my blindness – the things I don't see yet. And this must be the seat of my perception. Sometimes the scales fall away and I see so clearly a bit of the love Our Lord reveals to me. Each time He is able to fill my heart with that tiny bit, I get a little bigger. So the next time there is more space. What a gracious Lord! I know I will be a little less blind, a little less "little minded". One day I shall know – "even as I am known."

With new eyes I fell in love with the Lord all over again, yet the ditch still loomed. I failed so often. My self-righteousness was especially mean. As Jesus led me towards all that separated me from Him, those murky waters seemed bottomless. If I fell in, I might not be able to look at myself or Him in the mirror again. Wasn't it just easier to hope that good deeds would redeem me? I had a pretty good idea of my own shortcomings. But like a runoff ditch they always cut deeper within my soul. Sometimes I felt pretty good about myself – didn't God want me to? No. His desire was for me to live in the light of His Truth. My own self-image was hopelessly disordered.

I asked the Lord to show me how He looked at my ditch. Recognizing wrongdoing and feeling guilt are appropriate. However, my version of the ditch was damnation. It was accusation. It was despair. I was never going to be "good enough". And so like Eve, I was afraid. I know now that my attempt at confessing my sins was really a desperate search for fig leaves to hide behind. Fear must be confronted first.

I took my faith into two hands and asked God to show me my sin. I wanted His perspective so that I would never have to hide from Him again. During this time I spent sessions with Max at the bottom of the ravine. As our partnership grew and my patience increased, he became willing to trust me if I crossed first. With quivering muscles and rolling eyes he crouched. He lunged and shot straight into the air. I could see how hard it was for him to make that leap. I was so excited I barely got out of the way in time!

After many months of asking the Lord to answer my request, He did. In His wisdom, he took me apart much like the layers of an onion. He showed me how fear gave birth to anger. I realized that anger drove much of my life and my decisions whether I was aware of it or not. And then the last layer turned out to be pride. Very clearly, I saw how a distorted pride kept me afraid, kept me from an open relationship with the Lord. The passage from Philippians 2 came to mind: "*Have among you the same attitude that is also yours in Christ Jesus, Who, though he was in the form of God did not regard equality with God something to be grasped. Rather, he emptied himself, taking the form of a slave...*"

The Lord said, "You read this passage as if you are on the outside looking in. You honor me for my sacrifice. However, you must do the same thing. Quit looking through the window and enter into my utter surrender."

In a funny way I needed to say, "And Harriet, not deeming that it was important that she should be grasped, but emptied herself...." I must spiritually and physically do what Jesus did. I call it free falling. I do not grasp my failures any more than my accomplishments. To quote part of a poem,

> *All my life's plan is Thy molding, not one*
> *single choice be mine. Let me answer*
> *unrepining, Father not my will but Thine.*
> *("Disappointment" by Edith Lillian Young)*

I made an astonishing discovery. What was beyond the last layer of pride? It was laughter. For all the fear and anger were just silly distractions. They were straw men in the hands of the all powerful God. I looked at all of it and found that nothing was beyond His love. And I laughed.

God changed my perspective because He loved me through sin – He loved me over the ditch. And I realized that if I could spend the rest of my life pleasing Him it wouldn't be too much. There would be other ditches to cross for I am a fallen person. I yield to impatience, mistrust and laziness. This is a short list of my pitfalls. But I trust Him for my examination of conscience. I am not afraid to cross whatever chasm yawns before me. I discovered that "he who is forgiven much loves much."

I am not trying to write a treatise on theology. This is a story about perception. And there is a happy ending. After working on myself and my horse language, Max got to where he would leap over the ditch whenever I asked him. (And any other ditch we met on our travels.)

His flight level has decreased dramatically as he trusts me more with the likes of alien hay rolls, freeways, hornet's nests and new habitat. He is still not too sure about the goats. We're working on that.

Questions to Ponder:

1. How do I perceive my relationship with God? Do I want to be transparent to Him?
2. Do I have a sensible idea of my conscience? Do I review it consistently? Do I allow it to be formed and reformed? Does it affect my actions?
3. How do I respond to the "ditches" of life? Do I use God's perception or my own? What is the difference and what difference does it make in the crossing?
4. How do I deal with my past? How does it shape my present perceptions and actions? Can God do anything with it?
5. What relationship do anger and pride have with my motivations?

## Act of Contrition

O my God, I am heartily sorry for having offended You and I detest all my sins, because I dread the loss of heaven and the pains of hell, but most of all because they offend you, my God, who are all good and deserving of all my love. I firmly resolve, with the help of your grace, to confess my sins, to do penance and to amend my life.

## Lesson 4 - Centering

As explained in my introduction, the round pen is a training device. This book isn't meant to teach the value of that training device – I am not qualified by any means to do so. But there are aspects of it that pertain to my spiritual life which God has used in illuminating our relationship.

When I first started using the round pen, the effect was revolutionary. Max was "at liberty". No halter and lead rope tied him to me. Like a teenager with a driver's license, Max knew that I had no power over him. He ran around the perimeter and kicked up his heels. I have to admit it was exhilarating for both of us. If Max was going to listen to me, it would be by desire. He had yet to learn that the center of the pen was the goal. It is the place where he could rest. If I had gained any communicative skills now was the test. I stood calmly and waited.

As Max careened around the pen with an evil
gleam in his eye, I read his body language. His nose tilted
skyward on a tense neck. The key to getting his attention
was to make him run. If he slowed down I encouraged him
to speed up by crouching and looking at his hind
quarters. This tells him to go. To slow him down I stared
at his neck and front quarters. His eye never left me. My
task was to interpret Max's body language. I needed to
know when he was tired and willing to come into the
center. This is very important because it is the first sign
that a horse wants you as leader of the partnership.

Max was a very independent horse. He was not
going to give me respect easily. As I watched him, the
telltale signs of surrender began to manifest. First, his
inside ear flicked toward me and held steady. He was
asking to come in. A little later he started licking and
chewing – a sign of trust. Bit by bit his head lowered and
his neck relaxed. Satisfied that Max was listening, I tilted
my head ever so slightly and looked at his hind quarters.
This disengaged them and told Max to come in. My
companion, thankful now, trotted towards me and
stopped.

The center of the round pen represents comfort,
stability, reassurance and obedience. Here Max could
relax and enjoy my company. He said, with a smile, "What

a good boy I am!" Once he learned how to smile, it was his favorite expression to display those large, pearly whites.

The round pen was a microcosm of my life. What Max learned there about liberty and obedience mirrored my relationship with God. The image I recalled from scripture was when Jesus appeared before his disciples in the upper room. He had been crucified and was now raised. He walked through the door and said, "Peace be with you."

Here were a group of men who were frightened. Each had disappointed Jesus in some way. One denied him, all scattered except John. Thomas the doubter wasn't there. Even if they were fixed in their chairs, mentally they were running. Yet Jesus invited them to the center, Himself, with an invitation of Peace. I realized that there was a chair for me in that upper room. Hence there is a "Peace be with you" from Jesus for me. No matter what I had ever done, there was forgiveness. There was peace.

So out of respect for Max, I taught him to do my will by giving him freedom – he has no halter or rope on him. I ask for obedience. I let him run to get away from me. Yet I bring him to me in love and gratitude when he stops being wild and difficult. I wait for him to trust.

God waited for me at the center. Out of respect for me, He let me run around the globe in the folly and exuberance of my will. When I realized that I had been chasing my tail, I began to look at the center. The Lord was there with His "Peace be with you."

I imagined Him reading my body language in order to see the cocked ear as I strained to hear His voice. I licked my lips hungry for His Word, His comfort, His food – in other words, the hand that is always open for me to receive good things. My bowed head, finally, agreed that I cannot live without Him. If I maintained my unbridled arrogance, I was doomed to the circle of the round pen forever. The way out was the center. And at the center, is my Lover, the crucified Christ who gave up everything for me.

Another very vital lesson I learned from Max was the two eyes rule. Even if Max obeyed the command to come in, if he came in at a slant with only one eye trained on me, I didn't really have his obedience. If a horse gives you one eye, the other eye is planning an escape. This is extremely important body language.

I was having difficulty with Max one morning. He didn't do on that day what he did so well the day before. I tried letting him run and he would come in to me when I asked. But not with willing obedience; grudging half attention was all he would yield.

As frustration bubbled to the surface I remembered some very important teaching. Horses have their own personalities. Like us, they have bad days and good days.

Sometimes it was better to stop playing and let him go back to his normal life. Or you make the disobedience as uncomfortable as possible.

How many times have I been like that in my Christian walk! I go through the motions with one eye on the world. I have one eye on my preferences and comfort. I have one eye fixed on the rubrics of God's law; the other eye is as far from His will as the limitless circle of the pen.

Just about everything you do in the round pen requires no touching and precise body communication. For instance, I asked Max to move sideways around the perimeter of the pen. Instead of complying, he turned his rump towards me. Max knew how to go sideways in his sleep. Even before natural training, going sideways was trained into him. So as he repeatedly turned his rump in my face, I understood what he was saying. Instead of punishment, I sent him out to the edge of the pen and let him do what he does best: run. Once he was ready to come back to the center, straight, true and two-eyed, we were able to resume our partnership.

God taught me that punishment was not what waited for me at the center of my round pen. Peace and forgiveness beckoned. However, my relationship with Him needed two eyes. When I had one eye on the door, it was as good as having my back turned. For one eye that is on Him has no depth perception. It is chained to the eye that is running away, distracted, disobedient, and surly. When I learned to train both eyes on God, I began to understand His Will. As importantly, my heart yearned to conform to it.

Once I learned to train both eyes on the Lord, I had the "depth perception" to experience the depth of His love for me. Prayer and Scripture were no longer a duty but a delight. At the center, peace reigned. As I delighted in Max coming to the center; so I felt God's delight in welcoming me home.

Have I got it all figured out? No. Lots of times I let anxiety chase me out to the perimeter and I spend time rushing around the circle. Like Max, I have good days and bad. But I still have a chair in the upper room. When I sit there Jesus says "Peace be with you". It takes humility for me to put both eyes on God. To stop my useless running around means I believe that He will take care of everything.

When I asked for two eyes from Max you better believe I didn't want to betray that trust. What a relief to know God is at my center!

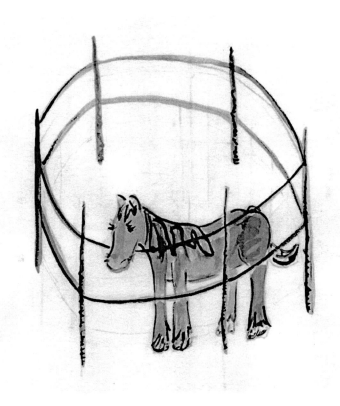

Questions to Ponder:

1. Who is at my center?
2. How much is God at my center?  Does He have both eyes?
3. Where is my other eye looking?  To what is it attached?
4. How do I run?  What do I chase?  How long do I run?
5. What will it take for me to put both eyes on God?
6. What chair do I hold in the upper room?
7. Do I hear Jesus' "Peace be with you" or am I absent like Thomas?

### Marian Prayer of the Heart

Give us a heart as beautiful, pure,

and spotless as yours.

A heart like yours,

so full of love and humility.

May we be able to receive Jesus

as the Bread of Life,

to love Him as you loved Him,

to serve Him under the mistreated face of the poor.

We ask this through Jesus Christ our Lord.

Blessed Mother Teresa of Calcutta

# Lesson 5 - Adversity

Teaching a horse to back up is very important. By Nature, horses are at their best running and thinking forward. The **backup** is the best way to know if the "brakes" are in working order. In other words, it helps you discern your horse's attitude. If they are afraid or ornery, the **backup** won't be easy. Horses can use this tool against you – but more about that later.

Working on the ground, Max got so good at backing up that a single look from me would trigger the maneuver. I move a finger at him in a certain way and get him to back up at least thirty feet. He would do this at liberty, just because I asked. When riding, all I had to do was think "back up" and as this sent the message down my body, he was already responding. Although I haven't always appreciated it, God has employed adversity as a useful back up lesson for me. Many times I pursue what I call "headlong" Christianity and, suffice it to say, I fall "headlong" into wasted effort and time. God would put on the brakes. Sometimes He has used adversity to test my commitment to Him and my willingness to surrender.

From the time I was seventeen until I was thirty-one I was part of an interdenominational Christian community. It was my life. Like Horton the elephant, when I commit to sit on an egg, there I will be until the world ends. When I turned thirty-one, God decided to teach me the **backup** by plucking up my whole family and moving us out of the community. For me it was physical and emotional amputation. Circumstances within the group that affected our move were extremely wounding. Still, I couldn't believe God was taking me from the womb of Christian Community.

Two of my Christian sisters said things to me that helped me weather the storm. The first woman said, "Harriet, even if this is all a mistake, God can bring good out of it. He can fix anything."

The second woman was making small talk with me on her front porch, while we skirted the issue. Seeing the naked desolation on my face she was probably frantically asking the Holy Spirit what in the heck to say to me. So she said, "Harriet, God is a jealous God. Sometimes He wants us all to Himself. So he takes us from all our supports so that we can rely on Him alone."

It took me four years to learn that and many more years to appreciate the **backup**. I had moved to one of the last places on earth I wanted to live. We were dirt poor. I was pregnant with my fifth child and, suffice it to say, it felt like the end of all things. But I realize today that God must orchestrate the **backup**. I had to trust that the same Holy Spirit that drove Jesus into the desert was working in my life.

What was evident at first was that I was not thinking clearly. Like a frightened horse I wanted only to run – from responsibility, from pain, from fear, from life. I didn't really much care where or how long I ran. A few times I experienced that on Max when we were out in the fields. He spotted some goats grazing in the long grass. Trembling seized his body as he trained his eyes and flared snorting nostrils at the apparition. One second later he wheeled and ran for all he was worth. Other times it might be a giantic hay roll standing sentinel in the pasture that sent him racing. Most of the time, the item was not life threatening at all. Try telling Max that!

God just let me run. It was a desert, I wasn't going to hurt myself running into trees, so He let me spiral down to the bottom of my emotional drain. During this time my family anchored me to life. My children literally preserved my sanity (while at times driving me insane!). My friend was right: God did love me enough to put me completely, spiritually and emotionally, alone with Him. And it was at the bottom where I was ready to receive His embrace.

Slowly, I began to yield to the *backup*. Once Max learned to yield to my request, he began to arch his neck, round his back and collect his body. This collection is a prelude to the best and most athletic oneness a horse and rider can achieve. The *backup* helps the forward movement! It catalyzes collection of mind and body in the horse. It also helps establish communication between horse and rider. Likewise, for me to yield, I had to trust that God knew what He was doing. And as I did so, my circumstances didn't seem that formidable after all. Life once again was worth living.

I have begun to appreciate the *backup* – and although I am not courageous enough or holy enough to ask for it – I can trust God to know what He is about when it is time for a re-check. God's *backup* helps me go forward in my Christian life with much better softness and yield to His grace. I don't like to wander about in the desert, but I have learned that there is abundant grace to be experienced there.

There is joy in the restlessness I experience one week or another. It is meant to drive me to seek God's will. There is joy in the unexpected hardship. It is meant to drive me to my knees and review what really matters: eternal life.

There is joy in the wounding of our souls and feelings: it unites us as nothing else can to the wounds of Our Lord. And where else would I rather be than united with Him?

I think that there is nothing else that gets me angrier than being misjudged or being blamed for something I didn't do. Fr. Thomas Judge (founder of the Missionary Cenacle Apostolate) said so aptly, "We should kiss the hand that chastises us." These things "back me up". They reveal the thoughts and action of my heart. They reveal to me how my heart is aligned.

Since a horse moves most comfortably forward, Max had to learn to trust me when I asked him to move backward. I made the yield harder by having him back down a hill or into a narrow doorway. He didn't like it at first, but the more difficult **backups** he did, the more courageous he became. The trick was to keep gently pushing him to greater obstacles so that his confidence grew.

Our Father, of course, is the Master of teaching his children to trust. Sometimes it is with little baby steps. As my trust in Him grows, He allows me to face greater challenges. One way He has used the **backup** concerned my husband's employment. Usually the scenario runs like this: no job, job comes unexpectedly.

On one particular occasion, my husband quit his job to start a business with a friend. It seemed like a sound business move at the time, but the whole thing folded in six weeks after much hardship. At the time we had our five growing children, and lived on a single income.

Six months earlier, his former co-worker had applied for a job at a large local corporation that handled computer training. She was offered the job around the time my husband's business venture fell flat. Well, life being what it is, she discovered she was pregnant. Since the position required a fair amount of traveling, she decided to decline the offer. Hearing of my husband's plight she went to the corporation and recommended him as an alternate. Within six weeks he had a secure job that met his skill needs as well as our financial ones.

I learned that the Lord always has an answer – be it orchestrated ahead of time – or one for which we must wait a life time. The experience of tiny **backups** helps us to trust Him in the really hard things that come our way. Yet I still find myself veering away from these tests. My inner heart says, "Lord I am afraid to say 'Increase my Faith' because of what will happen." So the most I can say is, "I surrender, help me overcome my rebellion!" or "I am comfortable, but please teach me to love the desert!"

Now Max was great at backing up. He had mastered the lesson and made an art of it. It took me awhile to realize that he was using the **backup** against me – to evade forward motion. If I am asking Max to trot or canter he starts zipping backwards, nice and collected! He used the **backup** as an evasion. For my part, I have learned to let adversity keep me from action. Wallowing in it, not moving on can become a wonderful evasion technique for not doing what God has in mind. What is a little frightening is that I am so very good at it. I made Max look like a saint in comparison.

So what is it about? It is what all life boils down to: surrender. I must surrender every single day to the grace and will of God. Even Jesus did this. He came to do, speak and die for the Will of His Father. The late Holy Father, John Paul II commented on John 8: 29: *"The One who sent me is with me. He has not deserted me since I always do what is pleasing to Him."* John Paul II said that Jesus knew he would never be alone at the cross because He did what was pleasing to the Father, His will. The Father will not leave us in the hands of death because the Cross is the beginning of the Resurrection.

This was the summation of the Way: surrender. Whether it is forward or backward, it was surrender.

Questions to Ponder:

1.  How does adversity or suffering test my will? Do I feel that both keep me from going forward?
2.  How does backing me up affect my trust in God's Will?
3.  Do I really believe God has a specific plan for my life? Can I trust Him absolutely?
4.  How do I use the backup to avoid going forward?
5.  How does the "backup" test help me become more collected and soft as a person toward the will of God?

### Prayer for the Cross

Dear Lord,

Help me to remember in these troubled times

The cross you carried for my sake,

So that I may better carry mine

And to help others do the same,

As I offer up all my troubles to you

For the conversion of sinners

For the forgiveness of sins

In reparation for sins

And for the salvation of souls.

Amen

## Lesson 6 – Lightness

The light touch is the ultimate technique when you are training horses. The light touch can simply be a look – not touching at all. When you achieve excellent communication with your horse *less* will always be *more*. This has been an outstanding way for God to teach me that most elusive of virtues – patience. To acquire meaningful communication with a horse, to be speaking the same language - takes endless patience, a soft touch, and infinite good humor.

Horses play games with each other to establish dominance. They also play fair. Instead of **Bossy** going up to another horse and kicking it out of the way, she uses phases of aggression. It starts with a look. If that is ineffective, the teeth bare and the neck snakes forward. If the offender is too dense or combative, **Bossy**'s big body comes crashing forward. The final phase is for **Bossy** to turn tail and let the offender have a resounding kick from the hind legs. Horses are so quick at this that these phases happen in seconds.

To teach Max that not only were we partners, but that I was the leader, I had to learn these games and phases. Max was used to controlling predators as well as the herd. He saw me coming with a chuckle I am sure.

One game was to teach Max to move away from pressure at a light touch. Instinctively, horses move *into* pressure. If a predator has its claws or teeth into a horse, to move away would spell death because a large chunk of horse could be ripped out. However, between horse and human, the horse must be taught *to move away* from pressure. This could be a response to a nudge from a leg, or a push from a hand. The phases proceed like this: touch the air, then the skin, and if that didn't produce movement push hard enough to indent the muscle and finally enough pressure to get the horse to give way. If the horse moves away when you touch the air, then your horse is really light and in tune with you. The harder you have to push the more baggage your horse has to work through. Or the more experienced the human must become!

Max, of course, was so tuned out to me that even pushing as hard as I could did not produce a result. He not only didn't move to the air touch, I had to get a hoof pick to prod him until he gave way. The counterpoint to this kind of training, indeed as with all training with horses, is that a horse learns that the moment he responds correctly and the pressure is relieved. For example, as soon as Max shifted his hind end in response to the steady poke of the pick I quit. Then I started again with the air, then a little heavier, a little heavier until I got the response. After countless attempts and many hours, I taught Max to respond at the hair stage. As I said, patience is a virtue.

Another game was to get Max to back up with just a look from me. Horses use their bodies to dominate. One way they do this is to push forward and move you whether you want to or not. They are so good at this I was constantly being moved and never realized it!

So my task was to stand my ground and give Max a domineering look to move him backwards. It didn't work of course. So next was to wiggle my finger at his face. He yawned. The third phase was to wiggle the lead rope attached to his halter. Max took all of this in with a well bred sneer. He even took some steps toward me but I was on to him now. The final phase was to swing the rope so aggressively that it became uncomfortable. Sure enough Max shifted backwards! So we went back to the beginning. After a few years, (I am a slow learner) Max would back up thirty feet with as soon our eyes engaged and I gave him an aggressive look. And after he learned to smile, he would always give me a big grin and say, "What a good boy I am!"

In evaluating my own relationship with God I was definitely a Max. With years of discipline, doctrine and self-recrimination, it was so easy to let any religious talk become just "white noise". I was a failure anyway. The only salvation I saw was for me was to never quit trying. At the very, pitiful least, I would never give up. To write this now seems so absurd! The Lord Jesus came to give me abundant life, not abundant guilt! At first He had to break me open – as I described in chapter one. I was a hoof pick person. But as I became attuned to His love and forgiveness it took lighter and lighter touches to bring me into communication with Him. Now that I know His Love, all of the rules and doctrines are love letters of guidance; I can't get enough of them.

Once Max learned how pleasant it was to move at a touch of the air, he learned to move just by looking at my hand! Once lightness was learned by both of us, it enhanced all aspects of our riding relationship. Max began to trust and listen to me.

The Lord's light touch is with me always, prompting me day by day. I am learning absolute trust. Lightness has also made me a more loving person toward others. Jesus' lightness helps me see the need in others.

When it came time for working with Max at liberty in the round pen, the phase training paid off. My body began to communicate so naturally that I didn't have to think about it. I could tell Max was listening to me, waiting for the command. We were actually having fun careening around the pen, then stopping to rest. He actually looked forward to backing up or moving this way or that with subtle pressure.

Rhythmic pressure is also a handy tool when moving a horse. Because it doesn't involve touching, a "look" is the lightest touch of all. It was delightful to spin Max in circles just by looking at his hind quarters. Because I was using his language exclusively, all of this made sense to him. In the end, I could walk anywhere with Max at liberty and he would come with me. He never had to be tied again for any reason, not even for his annual shots! I could get on him in a field and ride him all over without bridle or saddle. I could open and shut gates while mounted and he would even close the gate for me! Once the language started, Max started speaking to me and his sneers became a thing of the past.

It never occurred to me, before working with Max, that there was delight in being a Christian. I have always had a difficult time with the concept of joy. Most of my energy had been expended in trying to be perfect – on my own - and it is no fun! By learning to be a fun leader for

Max, I was able to understand the Lord's desire to encourage my own happiness. Heavenly things were no longer foreign to me. I now understood because I began to understand.

God has had infinite patience with me. He gives me the light touch out of love and respect but is certainly not afraid to move into heavier touches if I have my ears laid back and my feet planted. (I am learning not to plant my feet!)

The more I have responded to the light touches, the gracious touches, the more sensitive I have become to His promptings. His touch invokes no fear and cringing but only understanding and desire to be handled by Him who touched so many with just a look.

Questions to Ponder:

1. Do I respond or even feel God's light touch? Has my past dulled me to God's handling?

2. How can I become more in tune with God's touching me?

3. How can understanding God's light touch of respect in phases move me closer to Him?

4. Is my Christian walk largely joyless? What is the cause?

## Prayer

Let nothing disturb you,
Let nothing frighten you,
All things are passing away:
God never changes.
Patience obtains all things
Whoever has God lacks nothing;
God alone suffices.

*St. Teresa of Avila*

## Lesson 7 – Paying Attention

All seemed well with Max that warm September morning. He nudged me repeatedly with his soft nose. He knew well that he could distract me from riding him if he was affectionate. He didn't earn the title "smoochie man" for nothing.

"It's inevitable, Max," I gave him one final pat and tightened the saddle girth, "I only have two hours so we have to make it count."

In short order we walked down the trail and headed for distant pastures. Max ambled along, slack eared, as I dreamily enjoyed the sunshine. I remember looking between his ears and thinking how very calm a horse he was.

The next moment was unlike any I have ever experienced. I wasn't exactly unconscious but suddenly reality became a blur. All was gray as different horse paraphernalia whirled around about me. Boots, riding crops, spurs, saddles danced before my eyes. This was certainly strange! It went on for some time as I grappled for sanity.

Suddenly my neighbor's front door magically materialized as my eyes focused on the real world again. Her face betrayed worry as I boldly announced, "I've been flying." I then tried to lead myself and my horse into her living room!

Although I have never regained any memory of this experience, I was able to determine that Max had bolted and I had been thrown. Luckily, I always rode with a helmet. It now sported a significant crack. A neighbor testified that she saw me leading my horse across two fields. Time analysis suggests that my "lack of consciousness" had lasted twenty minutes, during which I blindly sought out my friend's house.

Needless to say this episode frightened me terribly. Faithful to the directive to "always get back in the saddle" I was on Max the next morning. Because I couldn't remember how it happened, I felt vulnerable. I was an experienced rider. I had state of the art equipment. Yet my horse almost killed me. My equine adventure had proved quite deadly.

This was one of the pivotal experiences that drove me into natural horsemanship. The unexpected consequence was that as I began to know the truth about horses I became even more afraid. *I was afraid of my former ignorance.* Despite all the training and equipment, I never understood the horse psyche or prepared myself to anticipate it. My ignorance was deadly dangerous.

It wasn't until many years later that I understood how this experience directly correlated to my Catholic faith. I had become a "cafeteria" Catholic. I had a wonderful upbringing in my faith, but societal trends and other cultural influences had seduced me into thinking that I could pick and choose my own truth. It had been years since I had even studied my faith. I was riding a horse I thought I knew through and through but once adversity hit, I was a goner.

It is still amazing to me how articulate the Lord is when He wants to get our attention! Here I was, at the seeming pinnacle of my horsemanship, just waiting for a fall! Here I was thinking I was an okay Catholic, and hadn't cracked a book about my faith in years! I wasn't a bad person...just woefully ignorant. I had ceased to nurture my faith. In the gospel of John, chapter 3, Jesus told Nicodemus, "*Whoever believes in him will not be condemned, but whoever does not believe has already been condemned...*" I learned from my accident that there is no stasis in life. If I didn't believe in Jesus and act on it, death lurks. I realized that it wasn't a matter of Jesus loving me or not – He always loves me. But I was in mortal peril by not paying attention to the gifts of the Church: scripture, tradition and catechesis. Jesus went on to say, *"And this is the verdict, that the light came into the world, but people preferred darkness to light, because their works were evil. For everyone who does wicked things hates the light and does not come toward the light, so that his works might not be exposed. But whoever lives the truth comes to the light, so that his works may be clearly seen as done in God."* Riding Max in ignorance was not going to save me from a fall. Willfully living my life with Christ on my terms was living in the dark.

As I had let my love of Catholicism grow stale, I became vulnerable to lies. One of the most destructive was, "Oh the Church is a bunch of old men who don't know what life is really like for us women." It led me into a serious breach with God. I had convinced myself that in spite of my apparent rebellion, all was right! But in His limitless mercy, the Lord allowed me a wake up call, a chance to say I was sorry. It was a chance to come back.

Pontius Pilate mockingly asked Our Lord, "What is truth?" Truth is something that can't be manipulated or ignored. I learned that dramatically through the accident with Max. I don't want to remain in ignorance any longer. I want to know the truth. Jesus is the Truth. It isn't enough to 'be good' and get along. One day I will face the Truth and I don't want to meet it in a trance!

What is the great equalizer? Death of course. I entertained death every time I mounted Max without really ever realizing it. Being ignorant of what a twelve hundred pound horse can do is just plain stupid. Being ignorant of where I am destined to spend eternity is likewise. When the Lord gives a wake up call then it behooves me to respond. I am so humbled and grateful for that invitation. As I delved deeper into my faith and the sacraments, I discovered how wise are the Church's teachings! To not dwell in truth is to taste dust – the dust I will become one day and not at Max's hooves!

Natural horsemanship brought me out of ignorance and into not only safety but the joy of partnership with my horse. In Her 'balance' between Holy Scripture and Apostolic teaching, the Catholic Church has freed me from a fate I don't care to contemplate. And that is to face my Creator with shrugged shoulders and a faint excuse, "I didn't know..." I am learning to pay attention and it is a matter of life and death.

Questions to Ponder:

1. Do I recognize the Truth?
2. Does the Truth direct my life?
3. Where does my ignorance lie?
4. What horse am I riding?
5. Who will give me the truth?

## The Golden Arrow Prayer

May the most holy, most sacred, most adorable,

most incomprehensible and unutterable Name of God

be always praised, blessed, loved, adored

and glorified in Heaven, on earth,

and under the earth,

by all the creatures of God,

and by the Sacred Heart of Our Lord Jesus Christ,

in the Most Holy Sacrament of the Altar.

Amen.

Sr Mary of St. Peter

## Lesson 8 – Looking Up

The pasture ended in a dense wood. Deep shadows wavered there in the stiff breeze. Beyond the gate a large dump truck stood sentinel. Max was certain that the truck was going to eat him. Every time we came to that part of the pasture, his ears pricked and he tensed to run. I watched him carefully so that if he spooked I would be able to stay on him. We both disliked that end of the field. I didn't know it then but I was actually the problem. By focusing on Max and anticipating his fear, I unconsciously tensed my own body. It communicated to Max that I was afraid. The thing I could not get him to understand was that my fear was of *him* and not the truck!

Two of my worst habits surfaced. The first was looking down at my horse. The old adage says, "He who looks down, goes down". I had to learn to look up and focus on my direction. Looking at the horse is a common problem for riders. The root cause is lack of partnership. The rider looks constantly to see if the particular maneuver was done correctly. Of course, it doesn't work. The success of any maneuver is in the timing, balance and feeling, not the sight.

The lesson for me to learn was to not look at my horse. I certainly wouldn't drive a car by looking at the hood! It must not matter if the bogey man lurked at the far end of the pasture. I needed to focus on a distant point past the problem area and "send" my horse there through feeling, timing and balance. After lots of practice, one day as we cantered past a fence post, joy leapt in my heart. We had forgotten to be afraid and I hadn't once thought of looking down. A whole beautiful world opened up now when I rode.

It reminded me of Colossians 3: 1-4. *"If then you were raised with Christ, seek what is above, where Christ is seated at the right hand of God. Think of what is above, not of what is on earth. For you have died and your life is hidden with Christ in God. When Christ your life appears, then you too will appear with him in glory."*

My gaze was transfixed on myself. Problems and shortcomings were larger than life because I tackled them on my own. The solution was to "look up" and seek help from above. By focusing on the Lord I gained twenty-twenty vision. As I submitted to Him, life wasn't so insurmountable. As I grew in trust, I was more capable of knowing what His Will entails. My walk with Him no longer involves fearing the scary end of the pasture.

My other bad habit was actually instinctual. By nature, humans are predators. We have our eyes set in front. When we want something we go for it in a straight line. If confronted with fear we clutch our hands and tense our muscles. When ridden, a horse feels the claws of a mountain lion. In order to ride safely, I had to reverse that instinct. Focus helped me over the fear. Partnership helped me conquer tensing in the saddle. What maintained my mount was balance, not a tight grip. What helped me mentally was firm discipline over my fears. I started to sing hymns in my head as I rode. I dealt firmly with my imagination. I turned away from all the things that *could* happen and concentrated on being a good rider.

Similarly, this helped me be a more mature Christian. Now that my focus was correct, I still needed to abandon old ways and habits. That requires turning away from fear of failure, rejection, and the future. I needed most of all to turn away from viewing God as taskmaster! It wasn't enough to look up to Jesus. As St. Paul says in his epistle to the Romans, my mind needed transformation.

My role was to release my grip on life. One day while in prayer I had a vision in my head of Jesus swinging me around by my hands. He was standing on a pinnacle and there was nothing beneath me. As He whirled me around sometimes the grip would loosen and just our fingertips touched. Then the warm full clasp of his hands met mine. He was laughing. This was my new life, utterly dependent on His hands.

Even years later I do not look down while riding my horse. It is much safer and more enjoyable to look forward! It frees me to be a better rider and better comprehend my horse's mood. I am braver, calmer and more relaxed in the saddle. This principle in my spiritual life results in a much more enjoyable Christian walk. I look forward to what God has for me.

Look up Max!

Questions to Ponder:

1. What am I afraid of?  Make a list.
2. Why am I afraid?
3. How can the Lord prove His love to me?
4. Does He want to prove His love for me?
5. How can I do my part to change?

## Daily Offering

God the Father, I thank Thee for creating me.

God the Son, I thank Thee for redeeming me.

God the Holy Spirit, I thank Thee for sanctifying me;

infuse into my thoughts, words and actions Thy grace,

so that they may be supernaturally pleasing to Thee

and supernaturally rewarding to me, forever. O Blessed

Trinity, abundantly assist me in becoming that which Thou

intended me to become when Thou created me, for in

that perfection I will give Thee the glory Thou desire of

me, and in that perfection I will find my greatest joy in

heaven.

## Lesson 9 – Baggage

I was very nervous. It was my first dressage test in thirty years. Dressage is a discipline that involves complex movements between horse and rider. Tests are choreographed and judged on a point system. The routines performed by horse and rider are executed in an exercise called "engagement". Very simply put, engagement represents the epitome of oneness. It means that the horse is collected under the rider and the two move as one. Max knew the test well. With my heart in my throat we trotted down the center of the arena towards the judge. At the exact middle of the arena we stopped and saluted the judge. Max was perfect. He went straight, stopped on a dime and let me greet the judge. A little bell tinkled and we were off!

Max and I did the test perfectly – that is, he performed each of the items in the routine. With a numb brain, I relied on Max's superior knowledge and experience to get me through. Turn left, circle, turn right circle, go down the diagonal...let him have the bit, bring him back to the bit, stop, back up...I ticked the maneuvers off. Finally, we came down the center and stopping, saluted the judge. I heaved an inward sigh of relief. No tinkle of the bell warned me that I was off course.

As I awaited the judge's comments she looked at me and said, "Is your horse even alive?" Dumbfounded I had no words to say. Kindly she continued, "Let's see if we can get him to *move*, shall we?" To my embarrassment, I was given a lesson on the spot! The judge was so surprised at our lifeless performance that she forgot to score it! Thanks for the distinction Max! Crestfallen and but holding my tattered pride together, we left the ring.

"Don't worry," my friend comforted me as I fought back tears, "She doesn't know how hard it is to move a horse like Max. Come on – let's wake him up for the next test."

I've heard it said that conflicted people carry "baggage". That is true for animals as well, I discovered. Max was fourteen years old when I purchased him. Many humans trained him, misunderstood him, neglected him and forced him to do things against his will. As a result he got very good at evading demand. Max simply retreated to his "happy place". He was a very strong willed animal. The harder I pushed, the worse he got. In the horse world this

translates to acute dullness. If you have ever seen a
person kicking a horse that just stands there then you get
the point. They are very strong and smart enough to figure
out how to outmaneuver most humans.

Max also knew exactly what he wanted out of life.
You could cajole, ask, demand or trick him but most of
the time you settled for what he was willing to give. He
was very highly trained in the riding discipline of dressage
and its skilled, flexible movements. But Max hated
dressage. He hated the arena, and he never budged from
that position.

As I continued to advance in natural skill and
knowledge, Max became a much happier horse. There was
the danger of using natural horsemanship as I did my
former training. That is, I left no stone unturned trying to
magically cure him of his mulish attitude. Part of the
challenge was to accept him as he was. For me this meant
I had to stop envisioning a horse that didn't exist.

It took many years to not only accept Max's
resistance, but to allow it to lead me into greater
partnership with him. I had to stop trying to "fix" him by
erasing his past. No, the past was what made him the
character he was. That was a bonus, not an obstacle.

It reminded me of Romans 5: 3-5, possibly one of
my favorite verses in Scripture: *"Not only that, but we even
boast of our afflictions, knowing that affliction produces*

*endurance, and endurance proven character, and proven*
*character, hope, and hope does not disappoint because the*
*love of God has been poured out into our hearts through the*
*Holy Spirit that has been given to us."*

For the next dressage test that day, Max came out
like a roaring lion, swishing his tail and grudgingly
barreling through each part. It was all I could do to hold
him and keep my own head together. Ding, ding, ding! I
had lost my place and had to be called back. By the grace
of God I remembered the rest of the routine and finished
the test. Max did his characteristic 'straight down the
center' routine and got high marks for it! But he was so
angry and upset that I had to face the inevitable.

I had to accept that Max was never going to be a
dressage horse. I couldn't completely fix his body or his
mind. I had to choose between the animal and my agenda
once again. It was tough because out in the fields I knew
of what he was capable! Was I facing a dead end or an
opportunity?

As I attempted to resolve this question, God was
mirroring it back in my own life. I maintained a dual
personality at best. There was my former life. There was
my today life. I despised the former me. I had left behind
an extraordinary relationship with the Lord to attain
popularity in high school.

I rebuffed former girl friends because they weren't "cool enough". I diligently avoided contact with girls and boys I felt would not further my ambitions. Popularity gave birth to many complications and compromises. By nature I am gullible and slow to learn. I had neither the wit nor will to succeed in the popularity game. My transparency set me up for put downs, betrayal and cruelty. I began to resent who I was becoming. Even though I hated my lifestyle I still fed at its trough. Deep down inside I regretted what I had done to former friends. Deep down inside I knew that by rejecting the "uncool" I was rejecting Jesus.

True to His Word, He rescued me. Yet the taint of those years crept up now and again to taunt me. My approach was to take a bulldozer and just sweep all of that past away. Hey, even a memory wipe sounded great! By denying who I was and wanting my past to go away made me a one dimensional person.

As I approached this in prayer, the Lord showed me that even when I was that despicable person, He loved me. Even when I sinned, I was that lost lamb for whom He was searching. There was value in what I went through – affliction had given me endurance. This endurance had given me hope because I could now see progress. My 'baggage' was not to be tossed off the train. Even Jesus kept his wounds.

He invited me to look at my past self and see it from His perspective. My immediate reaction was "Okay, dig in, Harriet and trade that image." I felt that God put up his hand in my face and said, "No my darling. I am only asking. I am not demanding you do this. I am always asking."

That brought me up short. Gone was the slave/master mentality. I discovered that by taking his suggestion, my suitcase of "baggage" became a treasure trove instead of a bag filled with regret and shame that could not be forgotten too soon.

Of course there had to be reconciliation for the wrong things I did. This is where the Sacrament of Reconciliation freed me to soar above my past. Like the layers of an onion, the Lord used this sacrament to gradually peel away the scars. The more I confessed, the more I desired to tell Him everything for which I was sorry. It was astonishing how happy I was now that my past was forgiven. For the first time I could look back and see myself as that little lost lamb.

Through natural horsemanship I learned to build a relationship with Max instead of formulating a plan to achieve my ends. Noting his proclivity for holding his lead rope for me or picking up things I dropped, I decided to teach him tricks. The book instructed me to go slowly and to use short teaching periods. Max learned every new trick on the first try. He loved it. I discovered Max's innate sense of humor. He taught me to not take myself or my past so seriously. Bit by bit, Max convinced me to allow him to live the life he wanted all along.

To my surprise, Max used his tricks to communicate with me in a whole new way. He wanted to spend time with me. I could tell he looked forward to my arrival. He sensed that I would no longer force him to be something he could never be. Max taught me to look forward to the life God had planned all along. I now understood His absolute love for me and all my broken parts.

As I made peace with my baggage, I discovered a new dimension of love. Because I could love my sinful self, I understood how to love others more. I appreciate other souls in a deeper fashion because I know what they can be and where Christ can take them. It has taught me mercy and forgiveness. I don't think there is a bottom to that suitcase.

Questions to Ponder:

1. How do I look at my past?  Run and Hide?
2. Have I let God forgive me?  Have I forgiven myself?
3. How can my past experiences be used to serve the kingdom?
4. How can my baggage make me holier?
5. How has my past made me a better person?

### A Litany of Humility

O Jesus! meek and humble of heart, Hear me.

From the desire of being esteemed, Deliver me, Jesus.
From the desire of being loved...From the desire of being extolled ...From the desire of being honored ...From the desire of being praised ...From the desire of being preferred to others...From the desire of being consulted ...From the desire of being approved ... Deliver me Jesus!

From the fear of being humiliated ...From the fear of being despised...From the fear of suffering rebukes ...From the fear of being calumniated ...From the fear of being forgotten ...From the fear of being ridiculed ...From the fear of being wronged ...From the fear of being suspected ...Deliver me Jesus!

That others may be loved more than I, Jesus, grant me the grace to desire it.

## Lesson 10 – The One Eighty

When someone talks about doing a one-eighty I envision them just turning around and going in the opposite direction. I would like to posit that just going in the opposite direction isn't necessarily a good thing. The one-eighty for Max and me meant a total change of heart.

As we cantered up the hill that morning the sun had not yet fully risen. That peculiar gilded light provided barely sufficient vision. As I encouraged him on, I felt led to say the "Hail Mary" in my head. No sooner had I finished when Max stumbled in full flight and brought both of us down into the dust. By some miracle he recovered and I managed to stay aloft. But we were both shaken and Max was dead lame. Chastened, I led my pal back to the barn; I had a chance to review my mistake.

Horses are made to move off their front end. This maintains their natural balance. Once you put a rider on top you have another animal altogether. To safely and comfortably support a rider, the horse must be taught to move from *behind*. To be more specific, they need to round their back, and use their hindquarters to move forward. This also dramatically affects how they carry their head and neck. I suspect that in a special way it affects their brain. They have to adapt their instinctual responses. This was the important concept I had neglected as I urged my steed down the path.

Natural horsemanship teaches the rider to do this by election as opposed to force. Once a horse discovers how comfortable this collection can be, there is bliss for both. Force can be used of course and gadgets have been invented by the hundreds to get a horse to change. I have used quite a bit of them myself and some of them really work. But they work to the detriment of the equine's mental stability.

Or, you can *ask* the horse to move from behind. This is challenging because you, the human are looking forward and ostensibly communicating with the front end! To put it simply you focus forward but *feel* from behind. You must know what the hind legs are doing and feel them collect underneath you. And you ask the horse pretty please to think from the hind end. If the horse is going to carry a rider safely this must be taught.

This reminded me of Paul's epistle to the Romans 12:2, *"Do not conform yourself to this age but be transformed by the renewal of your mind, that you may discern what is the will of God, what is good and pleasing and perfect."*

I realized that to try to understand God from my perspective (the forehand so to speak) wasn't going to get me anywhere. So I asked God to take charge of the one-eighty. Please Lord, I asked, teach me about Yourself. Ease my blindness, change my instincts, repair my desires, and teach me to be divine.

Max always had breathtaking power and collection when you could force it out of him with gadgets. The gadget's purpose was to give me enough strength to overpower his. He would arch his neck and grudgingly round his back under me. The whole time we both gritted our teeth while his tail swished furiously. Years later, I was able to ride him in the pasture bareback with no bridle. Max loped along just because he loved it. I never became an expert but could feel that the one-eighty for Max was lovely when requested and allowed in freedom.

My life on earth was "doing" for God - a battle between my baseborn instincts and the abundant life Jesus' held out. I couldn't cut and paste "Christian Life" onto my natural way of thinking. The Christian life must impel me from behind to move forward into transformation. For example, I was trying to change myself through self-denial. Now this has its merits. But it could only get me so far. And like modern people on diets, I would come apart. Self-denial made me irritable and despairing. It all depended on me.

However, I learned that the fruit of self-control is a different matter altogether. This fruit of the Holy Spirit is a gift that helps me transform my base desires and hungers. It impels me from behind with supernatural power. It doesn't depend on my will power, only my yes. As I yielded to the fruit of self-control I sensed a deep change coming over me. My emotions were calmer. My pattern of thinking and desires were self correcting. I am beginning to understand that in my life self-control will regulate all the other fruits and gifts of the Holy Spirit. I am eager to experience how God wants me to live supernaturally.

The term used for getting a horse to move from behind is called *engagement*. It's a loaded word to describe what happens when those powerful hindquarters propel the horse forward. Teaching it to Max was a slow process. It is akin to connecting dots. I got a second or two of softness in his back at first. Then over a period of months I advanced to a minute or two. Then the full impression of softness and yield ran up through his body as he reached under himself and balanced us both. No gritted teeth to "do this or else", no empty triumph needed. Because Max was so very well trained he understood the concept and once freed to engage himself, he did so without effort or resistance.

Self-control gives me the necessary patience to reach holiness. Whereas self-denial demands success, self-control fosters faithfulness. I can see the dots connecting themselves as I slowly but surely surrender my passions to the Lord.

Difficult situations are opportunities to flex my self-control and all the other gifts the Holy Spirit offers. Gratitude is the hub by which the wheel of my life now spins.

When I walk into the chapel on Thursday mornings and behold Jesus in the Eucharist, it all makes sense. I am *engaged* to the divine Lover and I can barely tear myself away at the end of an hour. To behold the beauty of the Lord and to inquire in His temple has bathed me in Hope.

I can see Max now, feeling for the bit, arching his neck and thrusting his hindquarters in breathtaking power. I soften my seat to his back and let the wind whistle by. He carries me on the air and I believe in that moment he sprouts wings.

Questions to Ponder:

1. In what direction am I going?
2. Am I a lifelong Christian that needs to change?
3. Am I engaged to the Creator?
4. Do I really understand the gifts and fruits of the Holy Spirit?
5. Do I feel that I live supernaturally?

## Prayer of Abandonment

Father, I abandon myself into your hands;

do with me what you will.

Whatever you may do, I thank you:

I am ready for all, I accept all.

Let only your will be done in me, and in all your creatures -

I wish no more than this, O Lord.

Into your hands I commend my soul:

I offer it to you with all the love of my heart, for I love you, Lord, and so need to give myself, to surrender myself into your hands without reserve, and with boundless confidence, for you are my Father.

*Charles de Foucauld*

## Lesson 11 - Obedience

As I led Max out into the arena I was sure I had fixed him this time. In those days I usually 'lunged' Max before I rode him. This is a common practice among horse people. The process is this: you attach a long line to a halter on the horse's head and have the horse move around you in a circle. To encourage him to do this you crack a long whip from behind.

On this brisk winter morning I wanted to warm Max up slowly so I allowed him to walk around me in the circle. I held the line and the whip in such a way that with my body I formed a "V". The line hand led him along and the whip moved him from behind. Max knew to a millimeter when he was beyond the range of the whip. Often it was difficult to even get a shuffle out of him. He was bored. Since there was no way I could reach him with the whip, he persisted in ignoring my vocal commands.

At my wit's end I purchased a telescopic lunge whip that would reach the rascal. At the right moment, when I wanted a trot (a two beat movement) I cracked it right behind his heels. Was he surprised! He speeded up immediately, ears pricked and gears running. You guessed it: Max figured out how to destroy the expensive gadget within three months. I didn't know it then but through natural horsemanship Max would go in a circle around me with nothing on him and no fence to keep him in.

The circling exercise Max and I learned had three parts. I *sent* him out, *allowed* him to circle and then brought him *back* in when I wanted. All this was done through body language. In fact, my horsemanship got very quiet after I learned this language. Before, I was constantly clucking, talking, babbling to Max to get him to go forward. Now, he just looked at my body and knew what was expected.

One of the things required for this exercise was obedience. At first Max was on a rope. Later we graduated to the round pen where he was at liberty. He learned to speed up, slow down, stop, back up, come in and go out all by certain postures, looks and hand signals. He even learned to come in the center, turn around and go back out.

At first I thought it boring to teach Max. I would twiddle my thumbs and plan my day while he trotted obediently around me. I was impatient with this particular exercise. Then I remembered another circle that always bears fruit: the rosary. Praying this helped me to play the game with my horse. I had forgotten Max was reading my every body movement. He knew when I wasn't paying attention. I ignored my end of the bargain: keep Max going by my own energy. Even when I was not touching him, Max could tell when my energy said "speed up" or "slow down". When I was impatient, I sent mixed signals. Down the road, when I was astride Max, this would become crucial to communication.

As Max began to entrust me with his obedience the game came alive. Here I was in the center, and a horse was doing exactly as I asked. It improved our relationship significantly. Soon I never again had to use a lead rope or tie him up. He hung around me and did exactly as I asked. He would follow me from the far pasture into the barn even though he *knew* I would be riding him.

Outside of horsemanship, my life was a big circle. No matter how much I ran around it, I kept meeting former footprints. How was the Lord going to teach me in my circle lesson? I was living my life merely to get it over with. Routine tasks and unexpected happenings were waves to get through. I thought to myself, "just get through this next wave and you'll find peace". The aptness of this image is apparent: waves represent an ocean. I don't think I have ever seen the waves stop! The Lord taught me the power of living in the present. The eternal was hidden within my daily circle of obedience.

So I divided my circle up into three. The *past* was my teacher. The *future* is my hope. The *present* is my true life as God prepares me for the eternal present I will someday live within. As Max focused on me to know my next command, he learned relationship and respect for me. My "routine" obedience to the gift of the present taught me to train my eyes and ears on the Lord so that my body could fulfill His Will for that moment. Here again the powerful prayer of the Rosary trained me to focus on the Lord, especially His death and resurrection.

One frigid day, since my arthritic hands were bothering me and the round pen was a healthy walk away, I took Max out into the arena to play with him. This arena had no fence around it. When I finally sent him out into the circle he went! Without any restraints, he chose to trot the circle until I told him to come in. I tried it later in a large field with the same result. Here was a horse that could figure out how to get out of any task, freely offering his body to my will.

Then being who he was, Max enlarged the game. One morning he broke the circle and went running off.

"Max!" I called, "Come back here!" He gave his characteristic chin on shoulder and then came galloping back to me and resumed the circle! From then on it became a game to let him "escape" and then come back.

As I grew in God's obedience, my life took on so many different dimensions. The present moment has become a prayerful dialogue even amidst the daily tasks. My routine has become an offering of prayer that enlarges itself everyday. Sometimes, when the Lord takes me to Himself, that prayer will burst forth in song. This is my offering Lord – the life you gave me. My daily routine has been eternalized. There are so many waves to wash through but the ocean brings its fresh water everyday.

It hasn't been simple. By submitting to the circle of my life, the Lord has been showing me how disordered my thought life is. The Holy Spirit transformed my "lunging" at the end of a whip to freedom. How empowering it is to hear the Lord say, "I want to bring order into your life." Instead of "boy, you screwed that up again!" That is God's work, bringing order out of chaos.

When Max was lunged, his life was looking down and forward, and goaded by the whip, he experienced punishment. At the center I was the taskmaster, the tyrant – do my will or else! In the circle of liberty I became a loving leader and my intellect a powerful friend. So Max looked at me, listened to me, watched me and finally obeyed me because I had something better to offer. I gave him his freedom.

Now I understand that the Lord, by teaching me the circle game, *sends* me out into the world, *allows* me to do His bidding, and brings me *back* into the center of His love and grace. He not only has taught me freedom, but trust, courage and hope. Life is no longer just "getting through". All of my actions matter.

Max never lost his love of freedom. And never was his freedom so apparent when it was submitted in trust. It became a joy to let him break away. I knew now he would come back.

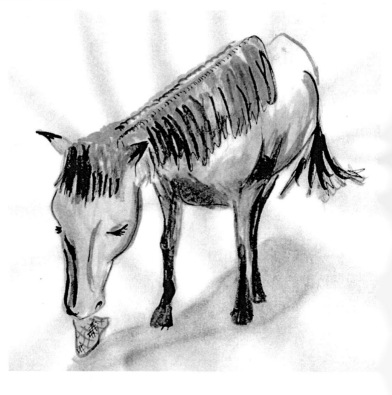

Questions to Ponder:

1. How would I define my daily circle?
2. How do I resist obedience?
3. Do the mundane numb me or energize me?
4. Do I just 'fill' the moments of life or live them?
5. How can self-control re-order my life?
6. How can my life become a daily prayer?

## Prayer

Lord Jesus Christ, take all my freedom, my memory, my understanding and my will. All that I have and cherish you have given me. I surrender it all to be guided by Your Will. Your love and grace are wealth enough for me. Give me these Lord Jesus, and I ask for nothing more.

Ignatius Loyola (1491-1556)

## Lesson 12 – The Breath of God

Whenever I enter into a relationship with a horse, I engage in a ritual I call "breathing his breath". Our noses touch as the horse moves his head forward and breathes in your scent. It is a quiet moment, this exchange of breath. The horse's breath is very sweet. (Except, of course, after their morning garlic.) The bond is exhilarating. I have often stood in the quiet morning nose to nose with Max exchanging a wordless friendship of breath.

I used to think that I was a pretty strange creature for doing such a thing. Then I found out that other horse people exchange breaths with their equine companions. The experience is life changing. When I first started a relationship with Max, it was that quiet moment of exchanging "breaths" that initiated our friendship. Max and I looked forward to that intimate moment each morning. I reveled in the welcoming look in the liquid eyes, as his nostrils pushed forward. His breath, warm and fragrant breathed into mine. In that moment you exchange the inner essence of yourselves. And although I knew that he was impatient for his breakfast, nonetheless I knew that he was glad to see me.

On Divine Mercy Sunday the Lord used this experience of mine as He often does with my equine adventures. Our parish celebrated the Sunday with Benediction, Exposition and the Divine Mercy Chaplet. Despite bad weather, I was grateful to settle myself in the pew in anticipation of being in the presence of Our Lord.

I didn't often have the opportunity to spend time with Him in this way, so I was eager. As the Deacon placed Jesus, in his golden Monstrance, on the altar my heart leapt like John in the womb of Elizabeth. I don't want to give the impression that I always experience Exposition the way I did on Mercy Sunday. But my soul burst forth from me – it responded to the absolute Power of Jesus Incarnate. I was so grateful to be in that place – somewhat like Peter during the Transfiguration. It was the Holy Spirit leaping in my womb to greet my Lord.

I can only describe it as the "Breath of God". I was so completely aware of His Majesty, His Purity, His Absolute Love that I couldn't do anything but weep. At first I thought perhaps I was so sinful that His Presence could only smite me. I earnestly sought forgiveness, as we always should. But as usual I had put the cart before the horse. I soon realized I was weeping because in that tiny glimpse of God – the merest breath – I realized how much I wanted to be with Him but couldn't be – yet. In His Presence I could only feel so very sad to be bound to Earth and this Life. I guess it was like a bird whose wings are clipped.

But the Breath of God did not condemn. The Lord reminded me that it was His breath that gave me life and His hand that fashioned me. And it is good. So like Max I took a deep breath and inhaled the sweet breath of the Holy Spirit. The Lord, in His Infinite Mercy, breathed upon me and invited me to take it into my soul and be forever transformed.

It was no accident that the Gospel reading that Sunday was about Thomas and his doubts. Like Thomas, in His Holy Presence, I could but exclaim, "My Lord and My God!" And like Thomas, completely surrender my anxieties, my weaknesses, yes, even my sinful nature, into the purifying, vivifying breath of God. I will never forget God's breath as He so graciously breathed on me.

Even as a child breathing held me fascinated and curious. Why did God create me dependent on the rise and fall of my chest? As I grew older I learned that the

Holy Spirit is "breath". The air I breathe is His province, the entry way into my soul every second.

Conversely, I catch myself holding my breath quite a bit, usually if I am anxious or afraid. When I have difficulty communicating with people I hold my breath. And the Lord has taught me that I only constrict His wisdom and grace when I constrict my airflow! Just as the body needs oxygen to survive, when I hold myself back from the Holy Spirit all those situations get worse.

Max always knew when I was holding my breath. He felt the tenseness in my body and trusting communication was severed. Then I lost partnership because Max started thinking for himself (survival) instead of looking to me for safety. However, when I was breathing the communication flowed effortlessly and trust actually grew. I learned that it was just as important to "exchange" breaths while riding as it was on the ground. A horse can feel a fly's legs when it lands on his hair – Max knew when I was breathing.

An instructor brought this tendency to the forefront. She told me that my breathing was too shallow, not to mention the fact that I continually hold my breath. And I saw the truth in that. Most of my waking life is holding my breath to meet challenges.

So I embarked on a program to learn how to breathe! The first thing I found out was that I couldn't take a deep breath! I had to practice, first by myself, then on Max.

So in fact it was with the Holy Spirit. I had to ask Him to teach me to stop, breathe deeply, and savor His truth. At first the deep breaths barely made it out of my rib cage. However, as I practiced and made myself continually aware of breathing, soon the breath reached far into my whole body and spirit. It required desire, practice and surrender.

What a privilege to breathe in the breath of a horse. It calms and nourishes the frenetic modern soul! I know that when I engage in it, I am very much in the present moment and pressing needs fall away. What a privilege to breathe in the breath of the Holy Spirit! I thank Max that he taught me to stop and breathe. Each breath is taking in the love and grace of God. If I let Him, then His breath will transform me, carry me into the eternal embrace for which I hunger.

Questions to Ponder

1.  Do I stop to breathe?
2.  What experience comes closest to the breath of God for me?
3.  Do I hold my breath?  How does that keep me from God?
4.  How can the breath, the "ruah" of the Holy Spirit transfigure me?

## Prayer to the Holy Spirit

Come Holy Spirit, fill the hearts of your faithful, and enkindle in them the fire of Your Love. Send forth Your Spirit and they shall be created and You shall renew the face of the earth!  O God, who has taught the hearts of the faithful by the light of the Holy Spirit, grant that by the gift of the same Spirit we may be always truly wise and ever rejoice in his consolation, through Christ our Lord.

Amen.

## Lesson 13 – The Tail End of the Horse

It was raining sideways as I heaved, coaxed and bullied the full manure cart up the steep slope. I said to myself, "Now tell me again why I decided to keep my fields picked up?" When I started this practice we were in the midst of a two year drought and the manure was solar dried as soon as it hit dirt. As a result my cart, even when full to capacity, was very light. I have to admit the sight of my pristine fields filled me with joy.

Then the rain arrived. It rained. It rained. And the sky let forth its sparkling, life giving drops to the parched earth. Wet manure is much heavier than when it is dried. Trust me on this. I also invested in a bigger wheel barrow so my trips to the dump site would be fewer. I had no idea how hard it was to push 100lbs of manure up hill and down dell!

On this particular day I was playing catch up. Circumstances forced me out of town for almost a week.

As a result, I was displacing about 1000 lbs of manure. Oh and did I mention that this practice gave Max the opportunity to play a game with me? It was his joy to upset a full cart if I gave him any distance to do so. I was scouting a corner of the field and my cart was parked half way up the steep hill. I turned just in time to see Max's big head shove the cart sideways. The manure cascaded down like a brown avalanche. Max nodded his head as if to say "Yes!" Then his inevitable naughty smile lit up my morning.

I didn't see it at the time but Max was teaching me even then. When I decided to keep my fields cleaned up it was to keep my horses healthy and to keep worms and disease at bay. I selected two convenient dump sites, ordered fly predators to keep the fly larvae in check, and found someone who would periodically pick it up for garden fertilizer. It was a pretty neat set up. All that was required was work and my old bones needed that anyway!

As I noticed a wealth of grass growing out of the piles it occurred to me that I could use this priceless gift for my numerous erosion problems. Manure stuck like glue to my steep slopes and promoted the root growth so necessary to permanent healing. Our pond had suffered lots of damage through the years from cows and the manure filled in the cliffs and nurtured new grasses.

Then I came across this quote from Augustine, one of the Church Fathers. I paraphrase, "A basketful of manure is not valuable on its own, but in the hands of a master gardener it is placed around the roots of trees to produce growth." Lots of times my life seemed like my manure cart – heavy and noisome. My cross is heavy as I trudge up the steep hill not sure if I have the strength to be victorious over my weakness. The manure cart represents all my good intentions and failed resolutions as I face failure and discouragement. Yet – in the right hands and the right places this cart produces such growth through the transforming power of God.

When my cart gets knocked over completely by a phantom called life – well, then I learn not to take myself so seriously! After all it is just manure and my failures are not so important after all. It is important that I put my hands on the pitchfork and cheerfully scoop up the scattered remains of my pride. There is victory in the "clean fields" of my daily life as the Lord transforms my "manure" into life giving growth.

In the ensuing years my vegetable garden and orchard rejoice over the nourishment provided by my horses, goats and chickens. The chickens especially love picking through the wealth of grubs and microscopic insects. Manure is one of the farm's greatest assets. So I have learned to take my failures and use them as a great asset as well. Without them I would not be on my knees. Without my weaknesses I would arrogantly stride through life believing that I provide nourishment and wealth for others. And my cross, be it the 100lb manure cart, a feather light infusion of love, or a wet nasty load, proves to be God's gift - His way of assuring abundant fruit.

Actually, collecting the manure five times a week has become a quiet time with the Lord. I am able to say the rosary (manure helps me contemplate my sin). Many mornings I am accompanied by a brilliant golden sun rise and roosters rousing the day. In the evening purple and red sunsets throw their cloak over the farm and woo the animals to sleep. So that morning as I trudged through the rain I did not begrudge my manure cart. But I made sure I kept Max in sight out of the corner of my eye!

Questions to Ponder:

1. Do I have life issues that resemble a manure cart?
2. Do I prefer to leave it scattered or tidily picked up?
3. How can the "manure" in my life be transformed?
4. Do I take my manure cart too seriously?
5. What scripture passages deal with manure and in what context?

## Prayer of St Bernard Clairvaux

Help us, O Lord, our God, since we cannot flee from the body, nor the body flee from us: we must carry it about, because it is bound up with us. We cannot destroy it; we are forced to preserve it. But the world surrounds us, and assails us through the five gateways of sense. Alas! Everywhere we are in conflict, everywhere darts fly against us, everywhere there are temptations, there are snares! Deliver us, we beseech you, from our enemies; defend us from all dangers to the soul and to the body, Lord, that at length we may come to your eternal rest, through Jesus Christ, Our Lord.

Amen.

## Lesson 14 - Keeping in Line

In the early days of my newfound horse passion I read lots of "how to" books. After being overwhelmed by one such tome I grasped the easiest thing I could handle. The author said, "If you cannot ride a horse in a straight line then you are not a good rider." Eagerly I saddled Max and went out to earn my spurs.

A few hours later I realized that it is *impossible* to ride a horse in a straight line. Frustrated and angry I got off because I knew it wasn't Max's fault – he just couldn't go straight! In the months to come I never did master the straight line but it haunted me. I would never be a good rider.

Years later, once I embarked on natural horsemanship I found out that predators are the straight line creatures, not prey animals. As I observed Max coming toward me in the field he always walked a serpentine path. It became very important to approach him that way if I wanted cooperation. My straight line approach from the ground signaled "predator going to eat you" to my equine friend.

Once on board however, I again confronted the straight line. Come on! I had put that behind me! This time I learned to *send* Max to a place instead of just concentrating on riding a straight line. This skill would prove to be one of the most valuable lessons I have ever learned from God. Thankfully, this course taught me how to accomplish it. Now with valuable training under my belt, I was ready to master the straight line!

The first task was to focus on a distant object. Then I had to keep myself balanced as I "sent" Max forward to that goal. If he veered I gave a small tug on the reins to correct his direction. I would say that for every hundred feet I had to give Max about fifty corrections. It required training Max to listen to my focus and to help him read my body language. Horses are really good at feeling a rider's body. In time, Max would see with my eyes by feeling my body direct him towards whatever object I focused on

It didn't take long for Our Lord to transpose this lesson for my spiritual training. I realized that going straight wasn't my strong point. In order to conquer sinful habits, untrusting attitudes and unloving actions I had to focus. I had to stop looking at my failures in these areas and get my eyes up and looking at Christ. He is the goal. When I focus on my failures I can't walk straight, let alone see straight. It takes trusting Him to let go of my familiar burdens. I have to believe the truth: He has set me free from them.

The first thing I learned while focusing on Christ was that I didn't want to let go of my familiar habits. To change, especially to attain holiness, required me to let Him in to clean house! I had a vision of myself lying on a slab surrounded by dense thorn bushes. The Lord wanted to get to me but I needed to give Him permission to hack down the thorny bushes. Deep inside I saw that my thorns were not my sin, but my fear of God. Better the devil I knew, than the transformation God was offering me! This was my first and most difficult step in mastering the straight line. *Be it done unto me according to your Word.*

All I could do was weep at my fearfulness and will myself to keep my arms stretched open for my Lover as He cut through the thorns with joyful abandon to enter into the deepest recesses of my heart. And there He found not evil, but distorted good. There I found laughter because what I clung to was so ridiculous compared to Divine Love.

Once He possessed my heart, the Lord began to teach me balance. The first lesson was (and is) very difficult. Jesus was more concerned with the "be" of me than the "do" of me. He loved me just because He created me. He loved me because I am. That is the first of my joys. Once I understood this, I began to have the balance and focus I needed to ride straight to the goal. Balance on a horse is hard to achieve. You can't ride safely without it. You can't ride as one without it. Freedom to approach the goal depends on this balance. If my "be" and "do" are unbalanced my Christian light is indeed under a bushel.

Then the clincher – I needed to give myself thousands of little corrections each day to turn my head towards my Savior. For instance, the passage, "Have no anxiety about anything" was something I repeated at least a hundred times a day. I slowly found that as anxiety began to wane assurance took its place. And in its wake the rest of the passage came into focus: "*in everything, by prayer and petition, with thanksgiving, make your requests be made known to God.*" (*Phil 4:6*). Then what happens? The peace of Christ guards my heart and mind in Christ Jesus!

As remorse, regret and repentance surface it is so easy for me to hate myself. God does not shine the light on my sins to condemn me – but to free me. Once I was able to focus on the truth: God hates my sin, but loves me – I was able to see the goal. But it took countless small corrections to keep myself going in a straight line toward the goal. And it isn't because I suddenly believe in myself – but I believe in Him and His redemption. Just as Max required endless patience and tiny corrections, I learned to give myself the same latitude.

One day I noticed that I was having a spectacular ride on Max. He responded to me as if he knew my thoughts before I transmitted them. We were having fun in the same field that witnessed so many falls and fears. I took him down into the dense woods and without even using my reins navigated the twisty turns, jumped the logs, plunged up the incline as if we had only one set of eyes.

Questions to Ponder:

1.  How is the balance of my Christian walk?
2.  Do I believe Jesus loves me just for who I am?
3.  Can I accept that He delights in me?
4.  What keeps me from letting Him in?
5.  What is my goal?

## Prayer for Guidance

Lord, we beg of you, go before us with Your gracious
inspiration in all our doings, and help us with your
continual assistance, that our every prayer and work
may begin from You and be duly ended by You. Live my
Triune God, so live in me. That all I do be done by
Thee. That all I think and all I say be Your thoughts
and words, this day!

Amen

## Lesson 15 – The Box

Something a horse would never do in the wild is to enter a cave. Inside the cave is a bear or a panther or wolf waiting to eat him. Closed places spell almost certain death so they are avoided. When you ask a horse to voluntarily walk in a metal box on wheels, i.e. a horse trailer, you are asking them to place their life in your hands. Yet humans do this perfunctorily every day. I have witnessed many distressing trailer loads. And it is all due to a misunderstanding of the horse's psyche. Max had gotten over this fear long before I got him, thanks to good trainers. So for this illustration I will introduce Sadie. She was a large, opinionated but gorgeous filly that wasn't all too keen on entering the box.

Usually, to get a horse to enter the trailer, you dangle a bucket of grain at what will be the head end of the stall. There is a door there for that purpose as well as a place to tie the horse once it has entered. At the rump end there is a "butt bar" that must be lined up and fastened for the horse's protection. My job was the rump end. I had exactly three seconds once Sadie was in the stall to line up the butt bar and drop the connecting pin in place.

I was always very nervous about loading Sadie this way but at the time I didn't know any better. If I didn't get the butt bar locked, she would be out in a heartbeat and probably taking my life with her. Enter natural horsemanship.

Once I knew how horses felt about the box on wheels, it made perfect sense to acclimate the horse in an entirely different way. Even though Sadie wasn't in my natural horsemanship relationship I figured that the method would still work.

The method desensitizes the horse to things they naturally fear. Narrow openings, dark spaces, dangling objects, blowing plastic are all things that put a horse into flight mode. It was important for Sadie to know that she could enter and exit the trailer freely. This would enable her to trust in the human who was asking for such courage. So I let her walk back and forth across the ramp, nose around at the little door, and generally took a lot of time stroking her and giving the whole operation a good and loving feeling.

Then I asked her to go in instead of leading her into the box. I walked into the adjoining stall and basically petted her in. When she came forward she was rewarded by soft touches and praise. When she abruptly backed out she received the same. Gradually the idea became her idea. To this day, Sadie loads peacefully and happily, no bribes needed.

It made me ask the question: what was my box? What mountain lion dwelled there? Why didn't the offer of holiness send me running in? My method of entering was to force my way into the box and slam the butt bar on myself before I could get out. This was the way I related to God. Once in the box a new problem arose. Because the Lord was in there, He wanted everyone else in as well! I hadn't bargained for my new life in quite this way. Sure, I love people. But people can eat you alive.

My whole life has been pockmarked with the scars of failed relationships. It took much desensitizing for me to want to love people and to serve them. I am a natural loner. It is easier to avoid the box – avoid trusting people and loving them. But as I grew closer to Jesus I saw what was in His heart and saw that it was the only way to true freedom. He didn't force me or bribe me into the box. He asked. He said, "Love as I love."

As I pondered this, He brought to mind my usual reservations: my memories of hurt and betrayal. And He showed me that I looked upon them as *rights*. They were mine. They were my reason for not loving as Jesus loves. I would lay down my life for people, but I wouldn't let them in. He asked me to give up my rights to any hurt. Jesus earned the right when He suffered for me on the cross. If I gave them to Him, I would be free.

It brought two scriptures to mind. The first was about the rich young man who wanted to follow Jesus. "What must I do?" He asked. Jesus loved him and told him he lacked one thing: to give up his wealth. Crestfallen the man leaves. His box was his riches. As Jesus asked me to love as He loves, I realized that this was my moment before Him. Would I walk away crestfallen because my riches were my self-protection? Ah – I saw what that man faced for the first time. Jesus wanted me to drop all, forsake all and take the risk of loving and it was just as frightening as that man losing his wealth. He looked on me *with love* and asked this.

The second scripture was when Jesus talked about the narrow way. There is a narrow way for every person. The narrow way is the box. But the narrow way is the exact width of the Person of Christ. To remain outside was to remain shackled to my self-love and that only produced fear and poverty. Wanting to be good was not enough. I must love as Jesus loves. And it was impossible for me to do so as long as I refused to enter.

One morning as I got into the car to go home, I heard a loud noise in the barn. As I rushed in, I saw Max cast in his stall. When a horse is "cast", it means they were rolling in the shavings and got so close to the wall they can't get their legs under them. This terrifies a horse. Not only are they in a box, but they can't run, they can't save themselves. Max was in a particularly bad way because he was in a corner and his head was jammed at a very bad angle. He looked at me imploringly to save him. Working on trust really paid off. When frightened, horses can damage themselves irreparably.

However I was in a bad position myself. I didn't have the strength to move him and any encouragement would put me in danger of his flailing legs once he tried to rise. I was really concerned that he not break his neck if he struggled. The miraculous event was that he calmly waited for me to sort him out.

I ran and got help and with two of us we were able to help Max get on his feet and out of danger. I think I was more frightened than Max! His trust enabled him to get out of a dangerous situation that could have ended his life. I remember the look in his eyes that said, "I'm not sure how you'll get me out of this, but I know you will save me."

That was a good memory. But it was Max teaching me yet again that trust is the only answer to all of life's hazards. It was so gratifying to see my horse friend trust me against all of his instincts to save himself. And to trust Jesus against all of my instincts is His gift to me.

Questions to Ponder

1. How do I feel about loving people?
2. Do I have a right to my scars and hurts?
3. What is my box?
4. What keeps me from loving as Jesus loves?

## A MORNING PRAYER

O my God! I offer Thee all my actions of this day for the intentions and for the glory of the Sacred Heart of Jesus.

I desire to sanctify every beat of my heart, my every thought, my simplest works, by uniting them to Its infinite merits; and I wish to make reparation for my sins by casting them into the furnace of Its Merciful Love.

O my God! I ask of Thee for myself and for those whom I hold dear, the grace to fulfill perfectly Thy Holy Will, to accept for love of Thee the joys and sorrows of this passing life, so that we may one day be united together in heaven for all Eternity.

St Theresa of Lisieux

# Lesson 16 - Yet

Max was bored. He hated the arena and here he was for the umpteenth time trotting around its dusty corners. Our natural horsemanship regimen was in full swing and I had gained a lot of understanding of Max's psyche. Yet, I had experienced a bad fall months earlier that knocked me unconscious and I was afraid to leave the arena. I knew very well that Max needed room to move and the tight corners of the arena were difficult for him to maneuver. But I could not overcome my fear.

Of course I have fallen many times in my career, but this one was different. I could not remember what happened. I don't know what sent Max careening over the pasture. I don't remember falling off. I couldn't examine my mistakes and correct them. The fear was insurmountable.

Glumly I took Max's saddle off and wondered if I would ever be able to freely ride again. "Sorry partner," I patted his nose, "Maybe next time." He laid his big head on my shoulder, content now to let me fondle his ears. He seemed to understand.

Then I came across a little bit of wisdom that broke the choke hold of my fear. It was a simple word: *yet*. If I added the word *yet* to my difficulties it changed the whole equation. *Yet* implies hope and success. *Yet* implies that the difficulty will not prevail. It reminded me of the beginning of chapter 11 of the book of Hebrews, "*Faith is the assurance of things hoped for, the conviction of things not seen.*"

The assurance of faith does not mean everything would always turn out the way I wanted or imagined. *Yet* it meant that God would see me through to His end.

Once I applied this little word to my fear the effect was dramatic. No longer was the pasture unattainable. Maybe I could take a few steps in the pasture. Maybe I could take one step toward it....and bit by bit with *yet* egging me on, I could tackle the fear.

I use this word to deal with all my horse problems. Instead of believing I will never get it right, I merely don't have it right ..... *yet*. Max and I graduated once again to fields, streams and woodland paths. Our partnership and trust grew one adventure at a time.

While on a difficult rocky mountainside, I learned that I could trust Max to find the way. Up and down vertical rock is not my idea of a trail ride, especially with hundred foot ravines yawning at my side. But "yet" had brought me to this point of trust in my equine friend. Max was actually having a lot of fun. This was right up his alley – no dull arena! And so even though at the beginning of the ride I was in terror, I just told myself I wasn't enjoying it, *yet*. Sure enough, the elation of conquering such a fearsome task lent me wings of confidence.

*Yet* has become such an important word in my spiritual life. It is from God. He understands my frailty and lack of faith. *Yet* it will come, one footstep, one decision, one faltering "yes" at a time. No longer is my sinfulness gobbling up my joy and hope. I might not love enough...*yet*. I might not recognize my sin adequately.....*yet*. I might not know God's will.....*yet*.

For most of my life I struggled with eating habits. I was an emotional eater and under certain circumstances still am. My laser focus on this problem bordered on neurosis. I believed that I would never stop worrying about my weight or doing without food that I depended upon.

The word *yet* gave me perspective. It also gave me humility because I had to admit I wasn't quite mature in my self-image. I had to acknowledge that I couldn't attain the image I had outlined for myself. I also had to accept that, in time, I might see what God wanted in all of this. In true fast food tradition, I wanted a solution, a victory now.

My acceptance of the word *yet* meant I was yielding my opinion to His. "Yet" helped me accept myself in the now.

Max never had an image problem. I think that inside he was convinced that even though his human friend bewildered him, I would someday get there.... *yet*.

Questions to Ponder:

1. How can "yet" diffuse my self-image problems.
2. How can "yet" give me patience with others?
3. Does "yet" give me hope?  How?
4. Does "yet" help me to trust in God?
5. How can I apply "yet" to my situation today?

## A Prayer of Resolution

Adorable Jesus, my Savior and Master, model of all perfection, I will try this day—to imitate Your example, to be like You, mild, humble, chaste, zealous, charitable, and resigned. I will redouble my efforts to see Your image in all those I meet and to be as helpful to them as I would be to You. I resolve to avoid this day all those sins which I have committed heretofore and which I now sincerely desire to give up forever.

Amen.

# Lesson 17 – Speaking the Truth

I followed my mounted friend down uncharted territory. As usual I was fighting mind games of sheer panic. Max was tense, reading my own anxiety. I kept trying to be brave, even nonchalant. To add to the mix, we had a filly following us. She was too young to ride and my friend was giving her an outing. We started down a wooded alleyway and came across a small herd of horses. Right away the tension level rose.

"Calm yourself," I admonished, "This is no big deal."

Ear flicking and snorts flew over the fence from both parties. Max was jazzed. He started to prance. The other horses were interested but not aggressive. In front, my friend kept calmly walking down the avenue on her large gelding, filly in tow. There was an embankment to my right so Max was about three feet higher than the herd. I was just obeying my injunction to calm down when the young filly stamped her hind feet peremptorily.

"Oh no," I groaned inwardly and took up another notch in the reigns.

She stamped again and at the same moment everything broke loose. My friend shouted, "Hold on – bees!" Her own mount had whirled around, feet stamping and the herd turned like a flock of birds on the run and fled the scene.

In a heartbeat the filly was gone amidst flying dirt clods and angry buzzing. My friend had dismounted and her steed tore himself away from her grasp and galloped in the filly's wake. Max was a wild mass of fear, muscles jerking and body straining to get away. He had not been stung yet but his companion's fear overrode even my feeble attempts to control him. I turned his head to prevent him from running away with me. But such was his strength that he shifted out of balance and we were inches from falling down the embankment and into the electric fence. I had exactly two seconds to dismount which, by the grace of God, I did. Max was a firecracker deaf to my efforts to calm him and to get away from the bees. The temptation to just let go fled as I envisioned him tripping on his reins and breaking a leg.

Somehow, my friend and I got back to the barn safely to see the two escapees munching benignly on her front lawn. Once again a catastrophe was averted. It was moments like these that made me thankful to now have a good relationship with Max. You can't always foresee or prevent danger, especially on a twelve hundred pound animal born to flee. And in conquering his fears with good leadership I learned a very important lesson from God.

That wooded alley was my life in many ways. It was sunny and beautiful but a drop to the right, bees underground, a flighty filly flirting with my composure and dynamite between my knees. Sound like your life sometimes? And as always, my imagination was my nemesis. It was *never* the case that my imagination gave me courage, optimism or strength.

When I discovered that Max had to exert himself to trust me against his own instincts and fears, I was ashamed. Here I was a daughter of God, afraid to trust Him for the situations I encountered. And it wasn't only my own life but that of my family and my country and even the world. The evil and hate can be overwhelming. The indifference and ignorance of Our Father's love is nothing short of devastating. But was my fear so very different from Max's?

About this time I read an article by another horseback rider. She talked about fear while she rode. But this woman learned to discipline herself to the truth and not to "what could happen". Because left to herself the outcome was always bad, always defeat. She realized that living in the truth of her abilities and training, she could have a good ride on her horse without calamity chasing their tail.

Many times at night I awaken with anxiety about just life itself. Where is it all going? What cog am I in the wheel – and am I doing what God wants of me to make His truth known. As I bathe my mind in prayer, at first stiff with fright and then gradually with confidence, I know that God is in control and He is love. Not syrupy love cascading over evil and darkness, but truth that offers transformation into wonderful light. In the gospel of John, chapter 11, Jesus admonished his disciples to walk in the light. To go forward in darkness will cause them to fall.

So Max taught me to speak the truth – the wonderful truth of Almighty God – amidst all trials, amidst all unknowns, amidst all joys. And the truth is knowing that there are no accidents or coincidences in His plan.

One night, soon after moving to our new home, Max escaped through the front gate. As I went walking down the paved road behind him I knew that it was vital that I not project the anticipated terror of a speeding car slamming into both of us. Just six months earlier an acquaintance lost two horses this way and the memory of it practically choked me.

With as much jocularity as I could muster I said, "Come along now Max, buddy. Let's go home."

He was disoriented and frightened. Since it was a brand new place and pitch dark, Max was not listening. Not helping was my new horse Sam who ran back and forth behind the fence, neighing nervously. My mind flashed forward into a hundred different horrible scenarios until I took myself firmly in hand. "Lord, please help me get my friend."

Max, finally recognizing my voice, began to see me not as someone chasing him from behind, but as a friend on which he could depend to bring him to safety. He turned and walked to me and wrapping my hand in his mane, I led him home.

Questions to Ponder:

1. What are the impediments keeping me from trusting God?
2. Do I let the truth guide my life or feelings?
3. Do I let events lead me down the path of despair?
4. How can I let God be leader?
5. Do my problems with trust have anything to do with what kind of relationship I have with God?

## Anima Christi

Soul of Christ, sanctify me, Body of Christ, save me, Blood of Christ inebriate me, Water from the side of Christ, wash me. Passion of Christ, strengthen me. O Good Jesus hear me! Within your wounds hide me! Separated from you let me never be! From the evil one protect me. At the hour of my death call me. Close to you bid me. That with your angels I may be praising you forever and ever!

# Lesson 18 – Walking the Donkey

Horses love to play with humans. In fact, one of their favorite games is called "catch". I have witnessed and participated in many hours of this game. Of course, unless you drive a four wheeler vehicle, you usually lose. And the game is most popular when you are short of time. Max was particularly adept at evading capture when I bought him. Prior to his purchase he spent a year basically standing in a stall at a college. So the freedom of the fields was too precious to be given up lightly.

One of the things I learned in natural horsemanship was honesty. Lots of times humans use their superior knowledge to trick a horse into being caught. I was never very clever at tricking horses so it appealed to me to just approach him with the halter and lead rope in full view. Because it didn't look like a carrot, Max got the idea. He showed me his heals and loped off into a distant pasture. I foresaw a grim afternoon.

Horses don't like bee line approaches or direct touches. They expect the courtesy of an invitation to draw near. To correctly capture a horse can take a bit of time for the untrained. Max was teaching me the first lesson in patience.

I learned from some donkey owners a new trick at winning the game. My four legged friend evaded my capture because he just wanted to be left alone to graze the green grass. The plan was to walk behind him and keep him moving all the time. It was very important to not chase or drive him – just steady pressure. If he stopped and faced me I stopped. When I took a step toward Max, if he stayed still and trained both eyes on me I approached. That was his way of inviting me into his space. If he turned tail then I continued to walk and drive him gently forward. Depending on how much time I had (or weight to lose), it was better to get Max into a smaller space! However, it worked like a charm. Once the horse lets you "in" you pet and reward him with a good feel. Since then I have never had a problem catching a horse. In fact, honesty has vanquished "catching" from my equine vocabulary.

This lesson helped me greatly in my spiritual life. I call it the "never give up" exercise. It is more than just perseverance. It is recognizing results. I no longer put inexorable pressure on my Christian walk to drive it forward, but I have learned to understand the gifts God has given me and how I react to his offer of holiness.

After all, what is my life about if it is not a continued walk toward eternity? Why would I not want to be caught by His holy grace? If I am walking through life with my hind end to God, subtly running from Him, indifferent to His will – am I not just a dumb beast? It is so rewarding when a horse – a new horse companion – turns to you and invites you into his space. They are taking a chance on the human. I have seen this in horses who have even been tricked and abused into being caught. They read my body language and take the chance to trust.

It still defies imagination that God would take the time and trouble to "walk the donkey" behind me. His patience and perseverance are such tributes of His mercy and love! In Francis Thompson's *Hound of Heaven* he writes,

> *Adown Titanic glooms of chasmed fears,*
> *From those strong Feet that followed, followed after.*
> *But with unhurrying chase, and unperturbed pace,*
> *deliberate speed,*
> *majestic instancy they beat—and a Voice beat,*
> *More instant than the Feet –*
> *All things betray thee, who betrayest Me.*

My role is Max's – the easier role to be sure. I need only to turn and invite Him into my life. I need only stop and train my eyes on Him to find true life, true humanity. Indeed, it is as simple as His Mother's Yes – please catch me and tame me and bring me to holiness.

Whenever I am performing a "walk the donkey" routine I can't help but focus on the Lord who perseveres in loving me. What does it mean? It means a change of direction. It means trust. It means wanting to be caught by divine Love. What was I running from anyway?

Bo the donkey

Questions to Ponder

1. Am I running from God? Why?
2. What in my life is more precious than holiness?
3. Am I afraid to be caught?
4. Do I fear what being caught might mean?
5. How can I turn and trust?

## Prayer to Become more like Jesus

God, our Father, You redeemed us and made us Your children in Christ. Through Him You have saved us from death and given us Your Divine life of grace. By becoming more like Jesus on earth, may I come to share His glory in Heaven. Give me the peace of Your kingdom, which this world does not give. By Your loving care protect the good You have given me. Open my eyes to the wonders of Your Love that I may serve You with a willing heart.

## Lesson 19 – Connecting the Dots

Max and I stood toe to toe. Or rather toe to hoof. His ears grew to mule height as he stared me down. Even though we were well into my natural horsemanship program and having wonderful results, there were still days of miscommunication and frustration.

This time I was trying to get Max to go sideways. I needed to move him with a rhythmic driving force, focus and my body. Needless to say, he was not afraid to pit his twelve hundred pounds against my hundred and twenty. On this occasion we had been at it for two hours and this was the fifth day of such encounters. I still had the mistaken belief that if you just did everything by the book, success would burst forth like the dawn.

I had to learn two things: Max was an individual and I had to eat the elephant one bite at a time. Most horse people call it *connecting the dots*. To retrain this animal I had to take into account his personality and also to ask and not demand. And not to ask too much all at once. With little successes came confidence, understanding and ultimately compliance. Well, most of the time!

To have Max move sideways without excessive force and in partnership mode, I needed to keep the lessons short and be content with the least little progress. In my own life I have never been happy with a little success. It has always been 'conquer the fault' and now, *please!* I brought this into my relationship with a horse who could care less about success. He just wanted to get back to the business of grazing.

In Max's rulebook, to cooperate required understanding then compliance. Sure, I could force him down the fence line with brutal force! But what I wanted to achieve was softness, willingness. Ultimately, I wanted Max to think it was fun.

When I dealt with sin, weakness or failure, I could only whip myself into a frenzy of introspection. Impatient and exacting, I mistakenly thought that God would be pleased with the thoroughness of my efforts. The only problem was that I never saw success or improvement. Each sin or failure put me back at square one. I never saw progress. It never occurred to me that God was pleased with any effort. Max helped me see the fruitlessness of this unbending ethic.

I learned that I needed to ask Max firmly and consistently and reward him the instant I saw even a shift in his body sideways. With much praise and petting I congratulated him on his success. That was all I asked that day. The next time he shifted sideways a hoof or two. Again I praised him and mentally patted myself on the back. So I began to slowly connect the dots. Each subsequent time I asked for a sideways movement I expected and got a little bit more. All of a sudden, to Max, it became fun and comfortable – not just another irritating task to get around. And I had to learn to accept the fact that there would be days when the 'mule' returned and I had to be happy with no progress whatsoever.

This has been one of my hardest lessons to learn from Our Lord. I have refused to be happy with the baby steps, the patient endurance of improvement. Because I expect instant success with my efforts (or should I say enduring success), only human weaknesses ooze from my self-imposed straightjacket. What I lacked was trust that God would see me through, and that my weakness was the key to connecting the dots in my own journey to sainthood.

Connecting the dots with a horse means asking respectfully and understanding the limitations of his temperament and abilities. Softness signifies the lesson well learnt. First it is a step or two, then five steps, then ten – maybe a day of no success – and finally minutes of movement and comprehension. It has taught me patience, mercy and perseverance. The immediate 'winner take all' approach just doesn't work. And as the dots connect themselves, there is a thrill of accomplishment, not to mention the added fruit of peace and companionship. The lesson becomes second nature.

Letting go and letting God connect the dots in my own life has let me settle down and not take myself so seriously. To be sure, sin is not to be tolerated: yet as I accept His reward for my little efforts I find I am not apt to fall into the same trap twice. I absolutely want to trust that He will get me to Himself. I have to let Him be in control of the dots. My prayer daily is "Thy will be done in me, as it is in heaven". As God uses my efforts to transform my nature, I have become confident the lessons will be well learned.

Two witnesses to God's fidelity come to mind and have encouraged me along my own walk. The first is the Blessed Virgin Mary and her Magnificat. The last verse says,

*"He has come to the help of his servant Israel, for He has remembered his promise of mercy, the promise he made to our fathers, to Abraham and his children for ever."* *(Luke 1:54)*

The word *promise* leapt out at me. God keeps his promises of mercy and redemption. His Word is good. And again in Zechariah's Canticle he proclaims,

*"He promised to show mercy to our fathers and to remember his holy covenant. This is the oath he swore to our father Abraham: to set us free from the hands of our enemies, free to worship without fear, holy and righteous in his sight all the days of our life." (Luke 1:72)*

If my heart is right and I earnestly desire His goodness, all my efforts are carried dot to dot by His Holy Spirit. If the dots are days or years apart it makes no difference. As did Mary, Zechariah and a host of those who have gone before me "marked with the sign of faith" I too can depend utterly on His promise to make me whole.

While learning to live with my dots, I realized that my scouring approach to saintliness could hardly be attractive to those who didn't know Christ. The Jesus I represented looked just like I did to Max with my sour face, demanding attitude and skewed focus. If I wanted people to know the love and mercy of the Lord – I must know Him that way first. I wouldn't say I achieve better than a few seconds or so most of the time – but what is a second in comparison to eternity?

Questions to Ponder

1. Am I too hard on myself?  Harder than the Lord would be?
2. Do I trust God enough to take baby steps?
3. Am I anxious that I will not measure up to God's standards?
4. Am I afraid to appear before Him?
5. Do I really believe in His mercy?
6. Do I really believe He will bring me to sainthood?
7. How can I change my attitude towards myself?
8. Does the Jesus I portray in my life hold any attraction for others?

## Prayer of St Francis of Assissi

Lord, make me a channel of thy peace,
that where there is hatred, I may bring love;
that where there is wrong,
I may bring the spirit of forgiveness;
that where there is discord, I may bring harmony;
that where there is error, I may bring truth;
that where there is doubt, I may bring faith;
that where there is despair, I may bring hope;
that where there are shadows, I may bring light;
that where there is sadness, I may bring joy.12
Lord, grant that I may seek rather to
comfort than to be comforted;
to understand, than to be understood;
to love, than to be loved.
For it is by self-forgetting that one finds.
It is by forgiving that one is forgiven.
It is by dying that one awakens to Eternal Life.

## Lesson 20 – I Am Not Alone

It was a gloriously scorching Alabama morning. There was not a cloud in the sky and the wind was brisk. I went up to the barn with a heavy heart. After a month of antibiotics, veterinary visits, poultices and everything else I could think of, Max had reached the end. I was moving in a dream as I trudged up to where he rested in his stall.

Only a mere month earlier I was joking with my farrier as he trimmed Max's feet. "Yep," Charles said, "Max has had a great life. He has probably lived longer than he should have with his disabilities. You've done a good job with him."

I didn't feel like that now. Despite everything, Max's pesky right front hoof – always troublesome – was now the size of an elephant's paw and the hoof capsule itself only days from falling off. With frantic calls, I lined up the back hoe to dig the hole and my veterinarian to put him down. Was it only a week ago that I thought I could save him? During that final week I knew I had to say goodbye to my friend. During that week, Max finally refused to leave his stall even to graze at the lush grass. He didn't even seem concerned about his best girl, Duchess.

I entered the barn and he looked over his shoulder at me. I think that was his favorite pose. I remembered one time I had just bathed him and lingered in the barn so that he would dry. I knew he would roll the minute I left! As I said goodbye and Max knew no more treats were forthcoming, he disdained the nice dry wood shavings in his stall. Instead he ambled out to the corral where the ground was muddy from a summer rain.

I knew what he was up to and called out, "Stop that Max!" He looked over his shoulder and carefully lifted his upper lip in a "smile". It was a trick he learned thoroughly and used it for a multitude of expressions. Right now it was, "Try and stop me!" Moments later he got up caked over every inch in glorious mud.

Now he waited calmly as I assembled every treat I could think of and brought some molasses water over to him. The past week had made him a skeleton despite all the food I could give him. He was beautiful though, my red horse! At least now he looked like the thoroughbreds from which he descended. I remembered how excited I was to trace his lineage back to the famous racehorse Man O'

War! I ran my hand over the soft hair and gently fondled his ears. He nosed me for a treat and gave me a smile. I had three hours to wait before the vet would get there and this would be my good-bye time. It was God's gift to me and Max's last lesson.

His poor foot looked ghastly as he lifted it to "shake hands". The peppermint horse treats had distracted him from his misery. In fact, he was eating the treats as fast as I could get them out of my pocket and running through his repertoire of tricks with joy.

It was very hot and the flies buzzed about. He didn't want a water spray; he never did like the hose. So I wet down towels in tepid water and ran them over his hot body. He seemed to like the coolness. He lowered his head and silently thanked me. I told him what a great horse he was and how he had changed my life. I thanked him for all the wonderful lessons he taught me. I thanked him for his patience as I learned so slowly how to be his friend. I thanked him that he liked doing tricks as much as I did. I told him that I wished I could save him.

In the gospel of John 8:29 Jesus says, "*The One who sent me is with me. He has not deserted me since I always do what pleases Him.*" The late Holy Father John Paul II explained that Jesus knew even in His hour of abandonment, when He was crucified for sin, that the Father was still there. At the complete solitude of death, and such a death, Jesus knew His Father was still very much with Him. Further, John Paul II said that the Father would not leave us 'at the hands of death'. True, I don't always do what pleases the Father as Jesus did, but my heart wants to please Him.

The vet's truck approached slowly through the tall grass. I prayed that I could keep my cool and be dignified for Max. In the end, God's grace sufficed. Max kept his calm, friendly eyes on me until the last minute. Then his suffering was over. I had ten years of memories and those last three hours to comfort me as I filled in the hole.

It wasn't until later, at Mass, that I understood what was Max's last lesson for me. He taught me not to fear death. True, he didn't understand what was happening – but he trusted me. I won't completely understand when my death comes – but I have a loving Father who will be with me every step of the way. As there was nothing I would not do to comfort my old friend and ease his way, so the Lord will ease my way with all the love and comfort that I need.

I went over those last three hours with Max. They were sad but full of love, care and comfort. There was nothing I did not do to prepare him and to let him know how much I loved him and would miss him. And that was just a smidgeon of the Lord's love for me! And I will be going not to a dark hole in the ground, but an unimaginable new life with no fetters, no fear, no looking back. And I wouldn't be surprised if Max was there to meet me and we ride once more – this time with wings.

Questions to Ponder:

1. Do I fear death?
2. Why?
3. Even Jesus died – how can that comfort me?
4. Do I have confidence that the Father will even be with me in death?
5. Do I even have a shadow of a doubt of His love for me?

## Mary's Prayer

I can hear you weeping
In the stillness of the night.
And I know your heart is reaping
Painful memories tonight.
But listen to the still, small voice
That never leaves your side,
To Him love was beyond choice
The love for which He died.

I see you turn upon your bed
And feel the empty place,
And know it mirrors all your dread
As the tears do on your face.
There is no arm to cling to
No warmth to feel secure,
No one to say, 'I love you'
So your fears may be endured.

Human are our needs for touch,
For speech, for love, for care,
What should be limbs becomes a crutch

We shrink when we should dare.

But He knows our grief

and loves us even more,

Fills our hearts with unmade peace

Pressed down from His great store.


Did you forget my sad, sad child

His love gave birth your own?

Or has solitude beguiled

What you have always known?

He catches your tears as they fall

And puts them in a glass

And drinks in full that bitter gall

That you might find love at last.


He says, 'Come to me my child'

My arms are open wide,

My love for you is boundless,

And ever at your side.

I will not ever fail you

Nor leave you in the night.

My thoughts are always on you

You are ever my delight.

H.S.

## About the Author

Harriet Sabatini resides at MaryGate Farm in Trinity, Alabama with her husband Leo, son Bernard and various assortments of animals. Her five children, two daughters-in-law and three grandchildren are spread over the United States but there is a bond of love there that cannot be ever broken. She is a consecrated member of the Missionary Cenacle Apostolate – a lay Catholic Order that seeks to serve as a missionary in the providence of daily life. A lifelong Catholic, though not always a faithful one, she rejoices in God's mercy and forgiveness. Her motto lately is to "love as Jesus loves" and finds that more than enough to keep her busy. It is her earnest desire that in these pages the reader finds a God of love and mercy. He is a God with 'arms open wide' and so desirous of enfolding you within them!

# Acknowledgments

Max, my red bay companion went to heaven last year 2009. It was his pesky right front hoof that started a massive infection from which he was unable to recover. I had the last ten of his 24 years and I don't think I will ever meet such an interesting character again. I am completely indebted to him for his patience, forgiveness and the orneriness that compelled me to be a better horse person and an even better daughter of God.

Thank you especially to my husband Leo without whom I would not exist, us being one flesh and all. It has been his constant cheerleading and speaking of the truth that has given me courage to write this book and to live a Godly life. I thank God for bringing him into my life. He did so much work getting this book ready – I could not have done it alone.

Thank you lovely daughters and gallant son for the illustrations! They, as always, make the book!

Finally, thanks to Cheryl Dickow, not only my publisher but my good sister and friend in the Lord.

Without her support and courage in giving me a voice these things would still be swimming around in my head! Thank you dear sister and may Our Lord Jesus always bless you and Bezalel Books.

Breinigsville, PA USA
08 November 2010
248951BV00003B/9/P